1974 Colloquium on Spanish and Portuguese Linguistics

William G. Milan
John J. Staczek
Juan C. Zamora

Editors

Georgetown University Press, Washington, D.C. 20057

Library of Congress Cataloging in Publication Data

Colloquium on Spanish and Portuguese Linguistics,
    University of Massachusetts, 1974.
    1974 Colloquium on Spanish and Portuguese Linguistics.

    1. Spanish language--Congresses. I. Milan,
William G. II. Staczek, John J. III. Zamora,
Juan C.
PC4021.C55 1974   460   75-28427
ISBN 0-87840-040-0

International Standard Book Number: 0-87840-040-0

CONTENTS

INTRODUCTION

The 1974 Colloquium on Spanish and Portuguese Linguistics, held July 11-13, 1974, was conceived out of a desire on the part of the Department of Spanish and Portuguese of the University of Massachusetts at Amherst to participate in a unique way in the 1974 Linguistic Institute of the Linguistic Society of America.

The format of the Colloquium consisted of three plenary sessions of papers in the areas of Contemporary Linguistics and Spanish Synchronics, Contemporary Linguistics and Spanish Diachronics, and areas of Future Study in Theoretical and Applied Spanish Linguistics. In addition, there were four special interest discussion groups in the areas of Spanish Syntax and Semantics, Linguistics and Bilingualism, Diachronic Spanish American Dialectology and Spanish Generative Phonology, directed by Mark G. Goldin (Indiana University), William J. Calvano (Temple University), Peter Boyd-Bowman (SUNY Buffalo) and James W. Harris (MIT), respectively. As a result of the success of the 1974 Colloquium, a second Colloquium was held during the 1975 Linguistic Institute at the University of South Florida, Tampa, Florida, July 17-19.

Of the twenty-one papers presented at the Colloquium, twelve have been selected to appear in this volume. Although Portuguese linguistics is not represented, it is expected that future colloquia will produce papers in this area.

We would like to express our appreciation to Jeremiah H. Allen, Dean, Faculty of Humanities and Fine Arts and to H. L. Boudreau, Chairman, Department of Spanish and Portuguese, for their financial and administrative support; to the directors of the special interest discussion groups; to all the participants; and to Professor Richard J. O'Brien, S.J., of Georgetown University, without whose valuable assistance this volume would not be possible.

WGM
JJS
JCZ

A SAMPLE OF SIXTEENTH CENTURY 'CARIBBEAN' SPANISH PHONOLOGY

PETER BOYD-BOWMAN

State University of New York, Buffalo

That certain systematic phonological developments in Andalusian and Caribbean Spanish, generally attributed to the 18th Century, may in fact have occurred much earlier in substandard speech, is evidenced in a number of private letters recently discovered in the Archives of the Indies in Seville.[1] Two of these, dated April 26, 1568, and a third dated January 16, 1569, respectively, were written by one Antonio de Aguilar, a fugitive from justice in Veracruz, Mexico, to his sister Ana de los Reyes and his wife Juana Delgada, both natives of Seville. The style and content of these letters, which the wife later submitted to the royal authorities in Seville in support of an application for permission to join her husband in Mexico, reveal the husband to have been an erstwhile bailiff and small-time shopkeeper facing imminent arrest and deportation to Spain as a married man residing illegally in the Indies without his spouse.[2]

Two of these letters (which we are appending as examples of the type of source materials utilized) were probably dictated to Aguilar's compadre Gerónimo Rodríguez or to his other close friend Pedro Belmonte, fellow sevillanos who had both emigrated in 1566.[3] The third letter was apparently scribbled in jail by Aguilar himself and then corrected and addressed by someone else. Both the first and the third letter are full of erratic 'phonetic' spellings suggesting that Aguilar and his friends spoke in Veracruz an idiolect (and probably a dialect) in which the salient features of present-day Andalusian and Caribbean phonology were already present by 1569.

Besides the well-known 16th Century merger of sibilant phonemes (seseo) exemplified by the spellings resibo, codisia, sierto, siudad,

1

siem pesos, el selebro 'cerebro', acordarçe, etc., there is orthographic evidence that the O. Cast. palatals /š ž/ had not only already
become the voiceless velar /x/ or pharyngial /H/ but that the writer
of the first letter confused the resulting sound both with the voiced
velar fricative allophone [g] and with the voiceless fricative corresponding to Latin F-: galapa 'Xalapa', guannico 'Juanico', enogo
'enojo', guntamente 'juntamente', megico 'México', trugo 'truxo',
digeron 'digeron', gerera 'Herrera', gaser 'hacer', gagays 'hagáis',
giso 'hizo', garan 'harán', garta 'harta'. Another spelling, carto
'harto', strongly suggests that this archphoneme had a velar rather
than a pharyngial stage of articulation at this time. [4]

Though the two letters happen to contain only one clear example
of yeísmo (ana de los reylles), we found several other cases of confusion in a letter written from Mexico City in 1574 by a barber from
Constantina (also in the province of Seville): cabayo, que valla,
valleta 'bayeta', negociayo 'negociarlo', va aya 'va allá', mas llierto
'yerto' que una tranca. [5]

The general weakening in Andalusian and Caribbean Spanish of
word and syllable-final consonants and the resulting confusion or loss
of /-l/ and /-r/, usually considered an 18th Century phenomenon, are
in the above-mentioned letters already well attested by faulty and
hypercorrect spellings such as foltra, folta, frota 'flota', bulra
'burla', dersirme 'decirme', arnascote 'anascote', felte 'flete',
selebro 'cerebro', puebro 'Pueblo', Escobal 'Escobar', me gorgaria
'me holgaría' gan 'gran', gasias 'gracias', compraadre (sic for
'compadre'), calde 'alcalde' quexame 'quejarme', vesto 'vuestro',
veracuz 'Veracruz' (twice), all indicating confusion or loss in
various noninitial positions. [6]

Loss of syllable or word-final /s/ is evidenced by the spellings
demole 'démosle', decanso 'descanso', decisey 'dieciséis', quedavadi
'quedávades', grande mercedes 'grandes mercedes', protera 'postrera',
bito que 'visto que', no . . . ma que 'no más que', esa mi señoras
'esas mis señoras', que tara 'que estará', mimo 'mismo' (with a
superscript s inserted later), and by the hypercorrected matalotages
'el matalotaje'. [7]

The weakening or loss of final /n/ (through velarization or possibly
nasalization of the preceding vowel) is hinted at in spellings like me
diger que 'me dijeron que', pogo 'pongo', em la 'en la', and
matalotagen 'matalotaje'. [8]

There are only a few examples of the loss of medial voiced fricatives: perdio 'perdido', plea nuestro señor 'plega a Nuestro Señor',
que 'quede'. But in another letter dated Mexico City 1590, we find
to 'todo', tos 'todos', and ahua 'agua'. [9]

Though statistically infrequent, 'phonetic' spellings by writers
uncertain of orthographic convention have long been among our most

reliable clues to popular (as opposed to standard) pronunciation of centuries past.   Lacking tape recordings of 16th Century Caribbean Spanish, and of the Andalusian frontier dialect of Castilian upon which it
was clearly based demographically, [10] we must in reconstructing its
phonology utilize every clue we have.   Just as today recent immigrants
to large United States cities (Poles, Ukrainians, Sicilians, Irish, Jews,
Cubans, Puerto Ricans) have a well-known tendency to cluster for
comfort and mutual protection with friends and relatives from the
region (and preferably town) of their birth, so from the very beginning
did Spanish emigrants to the New World, as documents of the colonial
period consistently indicate.   Thus when a colonist who could not
write (and there were of course many) wanted to send an intimate
letter to someone back home, it is statistically probable that such a
letter would be dictated to a friend or relative who spoke the same dialect as both sender and recipient.   This fact is important in evaluating
linguistic data, especially phonological, contained in the rare but often
highly revealing 'phonetic' spellings in letters that may not necessarily
represent the sender's own handwriting.   To be sure, isolated examples of some of the features noted here (especially seseo) have been
documented in Seville as far back as the early 15th Century.   However,
the letters just examined are unusual in that they reveal a phonological
pattern remarkably similar to that of modern Andalusian, in at least
some Caribbean area settlers, as early as 1569. [11]

APPENDIX

LETTER IG 2052, 6

querida ermana
    no se que es la causa por donde os aueys [acor] acortado en
buestras raçones y cartas. dende que estoy en esta tiera no e
vistto vna carta buestra. yo no se que es la causa de esto ni menos
ay rason para degarme de escriuir dende que estoy en estas partes
e uisto dos cartas y an sido de mi señora mari de gerera porque
sienpre me a gecho muy grande merçedes y gasta en esto me las
quiso gaser en cacordardçe mi (sic for acordarse de mî). agora
en es [ta] protera carta que el señor esteuan gomes trugo supe como
quedauadi[s]ermana buena y que guannico que lo quiso nuestro senor
para si. demole g[r]asias por ello y no resibays pena ninguna por
uida uesttra, que garta es la que yo por aca resibo de uerue (sic),
señora, de uos apartado y desde que mi conpraadre (sic) gironimo
rodriges b[i]no a castilla [e] estado en megico y puse tienda y ttuuela
puesta un año y me fue muy bien y con la codisia y deseo de uer
alguna carta uestra me uine al puerto de san Juan de lua, cuando
supe que la frotra (sic) auia uenido no me quedo maestre ni piloto

querida ermana.

no se ques. la causa. por son de os aueys. agora
acortado. En buestras razones. y cartas. y ende
que esto y en esta tieza. no e bisto. una carta bue
ta. y no se ques. la causa desto nimenos.
y fra son. dara. de gar me. de scriuir de nde que
es to yenes tas. partes. e uis to dos cartas. y ansi
go. de mise nora mari de çerera porque siempre
me a ge cho muy gran de mercedes. y gas ta.
en es to me las quiso ga ser En ca cor dar de
mi agora enes. pro tera carta. quel se ñor
este uango mes trugo su de como que sauadi
er mana buena. y que guan rico. lo que lo
quiso nuestro se ñor dara si de uno la gasias.
porello y no res i bays. pena. ninguna. por
ni de nuestra. que gar ta es. la que pora care
sibo de uerue se ñora de uos. a partado y es
de que mi con ora a dre giro ni moro dige dno
acas tilla. es ta do en méjico y puse tienda. y
tune la dues ta un. año y me fue muy bi
en con la co sisia. y deseo de uer al guna car
ta ues tra. me uine al puerto. de san juan de la
a. cuan do supe quela frotra auia uenido no
me que do maes tre ni diloto ni marinero.
ni pasagero que ch la fro tra uiniese que
pre care si me tra ya al guna carta. tto dos.
me dezian. que no y algunos amigos mios me
dijeron co mo os auia uisto er mana y que

ni marinero ni pasagero que em (sic) la frotra (sic) uiniese que
precure si me traya alguna carta. ttodos me desian que no y algunos
amigos mios me digeron como os auian uisto, ermana, y quedauadis
buena, y mas me diger [on] que no me dio poca pena de dersirme
(sic) que todos los mas dias os topavan de aca para [a]culla. por
vida buestra que no gagays, porque me days enogo en gasello. El
señor pedro de almonte digo que el señor frey rodrigo que era
difunto; dios sabe lo que yo sinti por la gan (sic) falta que garan a la
señora doña leonor y a mi señora doña guana y a las mas mis
señoras.

ermana mia y todo mi contento, yo tuve entendido que mi conpadre
gironimo rodriges os trugera en la foltra (sic) que estamos aguardando
porque yo se lo avia rogado y el me lo avia[a]si aprometido (sic) sino
cuando lo vi venir ya que casi la folta (sic) que dios salve se queria
gaçer a la vela y llego perdido que lo corieron franseses y le tomaron
el navio. el va en la foltra y con el, ermana, os enbio vente pesos y
perdoname, que os quisiera enbiar mas, mas no pude agora al presente porque conpre unas tieras en que se coge mucha cantidad de
mays. costaronme siento y trenta y sinco pesos y me la giso ayer
el[al] calde mayor de galapa que es un señor a quien yo devo mucho
y tieneme aprometido que en cumpliendo aquel cargo de galapa a de
uenir a esta siudad de la Veracus por alcalde mayor y si viene no
degare de ser aprovechado en carto (sic por harto) porque ansin me lo
a [a]prometido y a me aprometido de darme la vara de alguasil [6 v]
de aquí dedesta siudad de la Veracus porque ansîn me la dio en galapa
y la truge seys meses. yo quedo bueno y con mas deseo de veros,
señora ermana, que no de escriviros. en que (=aunque) agora a esta
partida de foltra y algunos dias de averse ydo e andado en el monte
disiendo que soy casado que por el caso me querian echar a Castilla,
ynpacado dedesta furia, pondre mi tienda aqui en la Veracus porque
ay aqui muy pocos ofisales y e sido enportunado de todos estos
señores de esta siudad que me que[de] aqui y ponga mi tienda y no
degare de ser aprovechado ya que entiendo estar algunos días gasta
que vengays porque mi conpadre lo lleva a cargo de traeros y el
señor Luys de velmonte me dise que (sic) mi señora mari de gerera
que degara de venir en esta folta que agora va y viniendo do ay con
quien, ermana, vos pudisidis (sic) venir y sierto me gorgaria (sic
for holgaria) mucho en que viniese mi señora maria de gerera por
el decanso (sic for descanso) y el bien de la señora doña Isabel porque
e oydo y se me a dado parte de sierto negosio que se [a]tratado en
este puebro (sic) con la señora doña Isabel. En la carta de mi
señora maría de gerera escrivo mas largo esto. a mi señora doña
juana y a la señora doña leonor le (=les) beso las manos guntamente
con la señora doña biolante y a todas esas mis señoras; y a las (sic)
señora juana de medina beso las manos; [a] ana de los reylles, mi

ermana be [so] las manos y le dareys un abrasigo por mi y que no la
tengo olvidada. a sus orasiones me encomendo y a felipa y a marta
le dareys un abrasigo por mi y por vida buesa que le digays a la
señora nuestra comadre que si ay falta de papel y tinta por alla porque
yo se lo enbiare de aca para que me escriva. a mi señor juan de
escobal si lo vieres le dareys mis besamanos y [a] Ana de agilar.
porque no tengo mas que desiros ni ser mas enportuno no digo mas
sino que plega a gesucristo que me os dege ver como y[o] deseo.
ermana, si uvire (sic) remedio vu (sic) orden para venir aca enbiamelo
a desir en el navio de aviso para que yo tenga la sertedunbre dello.
fecha a 21 del mes de abril de 1568 oy lunes, y quedo por buestro -
Antonio de Aguilar
Tachado: 'Petición de Juana Delgada para marcharse con su marido.
Se la conceden en Madrid 26 otubre-1569'

LETTER IG 2052, 5

señora
    por que con mi conpadre geronimo rrodrigues le tengo escrito
largo esta no sirvira pa mas de para que señora sepais como quedo
bueno de salud y de lo demas quedo como quedan algunos casados aca
a sonbra de tejados porque andamos huydos al monte por que no mos
(sic) llevasen en esta flota y a esta causa e andado desasegado (sic
for desasosegado) por que aqui envian mucha jente presa y maltratada
En yendose esta flota luego porne mi tienda aqui porque sienpre hay
mucho que haser y me yra bien con ayuda de Dios. por tanto señora
alla va pedro belmonte por mi señora maria de herrera por que el
queda tanbien ausente. Lo que señora os rruego es que viniendo ella
que vengais en su conpañía y cuando por ventura no viniese mi conpadre geronimo rrodrigues podeys venir con el por quel lleva veynte
pesos con que al presente me halle. Veni señora en todo caso por
que esta es mi voluntad que en esta tierra mos (sic) ira bien y no mos
(sic) faltara todo rrecaudo por que en fin son yndias, pueden los
honbres ganala aca mejor que no alla y en el navio de aviso que
viniere me puede escrevir como viene y que nao por que lo sepa y
todo quanto alla se consertare de fletes y lo que alla pusieren yo lo
conplire aca. a mis señores (sic) doña leonor y doña juana y doña
violante les beso las manos y questa ayan por suya. a la señora
juana de medina y ana de los rreyes mi hermana beso las manos y
a la señora vuestra comadre le de mis encomiendas y que por que
me a dexado descrevir, que si falta papel y tinta, y que mucho me
peso de la desgracia de calderon.
    señora aca me han dicho algunos amigos mios que os han topado
en la calle muchas veses. escusaldo, por que no ay alla cosa que pase
que aca no se sabe, y con tanto nuestro señor me dexe veros como

yo deseo. de la vera + a xxvj de abril 1568[de]
de ves to [sic for vuestro] marido
antonio de aguilar

LETTER IG 2052, 7

My señora y mi contento
   yo quedo qual dios me remedie, pues quedo preso y con unos
grillos por casado, y esto, señora, bien se pudierra (sic) aver
remediado con buestra venida mas no os po[n]go qulpa, señora,
porque bien entiendo yo no aver sido mas en buestra mano ni tengo
de quien quexarme sino de mi mismo pués de bueno que soi azen
todos bulra (sic for burla) de mi como mi conpadre lo a eho (sic)
de mi que a venido a esta tiera dos vezes perdio (sic) y lo e eho (sic)
con el como dios sabe y averlle (sic) dado sienpre dineros para daros
y (el) no averoslos dado. mi alma, por vida buestra y mia que agays
lo que os [e] enbiado a rogar en mis cart[as] en que v[e]nguays (sic)
aca por qualquiera manera que pudierdis, porque mira, mi alma,
no penseis que venir aca que es aora mun[c]ho, no es nada, porquo
en la era de aor[a] vienen mun[c]has señoras con quien podeys venir.
Yo paguare aca el felte (sic) y lo demas que fuere menester mi alma
no [o]s tengo ma[s] que dezir sino que ple (sic for plega) a Nuestro
Señor me os dege ver como yo deseo y quedo por buestro como
siempre.
   a desisey (sic) dias del mes d[e] enero. A mi señora marya de
erera lle escrivo mas largo y a esa mi señoras ta[n]bien.
      Antoni[o]de aguilar
         buestro
(con otra letra):
   A mi deseada señora juana delgada, muger de antono de aguilar en
casa de la señora maria de herrera en Sevilla a la puerta mayor de
Sant Marcos
   'Petición de Juana Delgada para marcharse con su marido. Se
le concede en Madrid 26 octubre 1569'

NOTES

   1. These letters, over 600 in number, were discovered by the
colonial historian Professor Heinrich Otte of the Freie Universität
Berlin among supporting documents submitted to the royal authorities
by seekers of permits to emigrate to the colonies. Each of the letters
had been used to substantiate the fact that the petitioner had a spouse,
relative, or patron summoning him or her to the Indies for bona fide
reasons. In the Archivo General de Indias, they may be located
passim under Indiferente General Nos. 2048-2074, Nos. 2077-2107,

Nos. 1209 ff., and No. 1374 ff. The work of transcribing the letters
was carried out by Sra. Guadalupe Albi for Dr. Otte, to whom I am
indebted for making a microfilm copy available for use in my computer-
assisted inquiry into early regional varieties of American Spanish
(LASCODOCS, or the Linguistic Analysis of Spanish Colonial Documents). However, in view of the crucial importance to this study of
the exact original spelling of the two letters cited here, I verified the
spelling by securing from the Archivo de Índias a microfilm of the
original letters themselves.

   2.   Entry No. 11,916 in the typescript of Vol. IV of my five-volume
Indice geobiográfico de 40.000 pobladores españoles de América en
el siglo XVI tells us that Juana Delgada, the daughter of Juan García
and Francisca Fernández and a native of the city of Seville, was
granted a permit in 1570 to join her husband Antonio de Aguilar in
Mexico, but I have no record of when he himself emigrated.

   3.   Cf. Boyd-Bowman, IGB, Vol. IV, No. 11,540 and No. 10,894.

   4.   Some more or less contemporary letters from Mexico City
show the same orthographic confusion, e.g. ygas 'hijas' (1575), rigas
'rijas' (1582), ajorays 'ahorráis' (1590).   Examples from elsewhere
are golgara 'holgara' (Lima 1558), megor 'mejor' (Arequipa 1560),
aventagar 'aventajar' (Lima 1563), me guelgo 'me huelgo' (Lima 1583),
gugalla 'jugarla' (Charcas 1584), higitas de azavache (Perú 1586),
agilaldo 'aguinaldo' (Panamá 1587), quegar 'quejar', de 'deje' (Panamá
1592).   In a letter of 1559 written by a sevillano in Lima we find a
curious transitional stage (possibly [ç]) represented by the spelling
<xi>: mexior . . . dexiara . . . moxiere 'mujer' . . . vexies 'vejez'
mis oxios 'ojos'.   This spelling was not, however, consistent, for in
the same letter we also found ixo 'hijo', viaxe, trabaxos, consexo,
and xuntamente.   Examples from the 17th Century (a small selection):
vesta (sic) muher y hijos . . . a quien degar 'dejar' (Lima 1604),
yga mía . . . las cartas que me trago 'trajo' . . . la megor ocasión
(Mexico City 1617).   A semiliterate miner in northern New Spain
writes in 1635 yo rrehistro, mahestad, San Hosed 'José'.   All of
these spellings point to a confusion, in some speakers at least, of
the velar or pharyngial sounds corresponding to O. Cast. /š/, /ž/,
/h/, and the new fricative allophone of /g/.

   5.   Fols. 7-9 of letters located in Indiferente General, Legajo No.
2055.   Examples of early yeísmo in letters from other regions are
cogoio 'cogollo' (Cuzco 1549), aiamos 'hallamos' (New Granada 1565),
balla 'vaya' (Perú 1583), and aya 'allá (Sto. Domingo 1583).   Two
letters written from Puebla in 1581 and already studied by Guillermo
Guitarte in his 'Notas para la historia del yeísmo' (Sprache und
Geschichte.   Festschrift für Harri Meier zum 65. Geburtstag.
München 1971: 179-198), show vallan 'vayan' hayares 'hallares',
salla 'saya', alla 'haya', and yamais 'llamáis'.

6. Further examples I have found involving confusion or loss of /l/ or /r/ when not initial: hazed 'hacer' (twice) (Puebla 1555), escursa 'excusa' (Mexico City 1558), groria 'gloria' (Lima 1558), mercadel . . . mercadeles (Lima 1558), praziendo . . . frotra . . . provres 'plaziendo . . . flota . . . pobres' (Arequipa 1560), veso servido 'vuestro servidor' (Arequipa 1560), rrepatimiento 'reparti-miento' (Quito 1560), sin onden 'sin orden' (Panamá 1560), mi seño 'mi señor' (Venezuela 1564), hizien 'hizieran' (Cuzco 1566), qunpra . . . qunprera . . . obrigado . . . obrigar . . . fretes . . . frota 'cumpla . . . cumpliera', etc. (Mexico City 1574, the writer being a tanner from Zafra, Badajoz), estra . . . estrotra 'esta . . . estotra' (Mexico City 1574), llelgo 'llegó' (Mexico City 1575), perscrbero 'persevero' (Mexico 1575), huefanos 'huérfanos' (Perú 1577), diligida 'dirigida' (Lima 1580), quedame 'quedarme' (Potosí 1580), hacel 'hacer' (Puebla 1581), muje 'mujer' (Quito 1582), Panamar 'Panamá' (twice) (Panamá 1582), agoa 'agora' (Mexico 1582), conosce 'conocer' (Sto. Domingo 1583), esquimada 'esquilmada' (Puebla 1583), mercadel (Lima 1584), Guayaqui 'Guayaquil' (Quito 1586), Tunjar 'Tunja' and no puedo olvidad (sic) (Tunja 1587), huerbo 'vuelvo' and the hypercorrect nobrienbre (Sto. Domingo 1589), Almonacil 'Almonacid' and prayertado 'proyectado' (Veracruz 1589), corcha 'colcha' (Perú 1589), pudie 'pudiere' (Perú 1590), comenar 'colmenar' and alquile 'alquiler' (Cartagena 1590), sufir 'sufrir' (Habana 1591), mercadel and Rodrigo de Verge 'Verguer' (Panamá 1592), alaldes (sic) 'hallardes' (Panamá 1592), reçertor 'receptor' (Mexico City 1593), refigerio 'refrigerio' (Mexico City 1594), alquile 'alquiler' (Honduras 1598), añir 'añil' (Honduras 1599), taiendolos 'trayéndolos' . . . albiertan 'adviertan' (Guatemala 1600), vesta muher (sic) (Lima 1604), favo 'favor', ycio 'Ircio', ago 'algo' and crerigo 'clérigo' (Mexico City 1617). Many of these examples are taken from letters written by colonists from Seville. We even found an early example of assibilation: quesido 'querido' (Lima 1586).

7. Epistolary signals of loss of /s/ elsewhere at about this period are: los quale (Tehuantepec 1556), los que . . . soy 'sois' (Arequipa 1560), os partiria 'partirías' (Arequipa 1560), vos enbiaste 'enviasteis' (Panamá 1560), monarterio 'monasterio' (Panamá 1560), aparesjo 'aparejo' (Quito 1560), ata agora 'hasta ahora' (Lima 1561), los cientos y nueve pesos (a hypercorrection from Lima 1561), los bueno 'los buenos' and no enbio recasdo 'recado' (Panamá 1563), dos hijos suyo (Mexico City 1564), se viniese los (=lo) mas breve que ser pudiese (Chile 1564), las cartas . . . son esta 'éstas' (Chile 1564), escriville (a vuestras mercedes) (Panamá 1568), manifertar 'mani-festar' (Potosí 1573), es amigo mio y no 'nos' tratamos de tales (Cartagena 1575), muger . . . cosdiciosa (hypercorrect for codiciosa) and tantas jente vienen (Lima 1576), cada seis dia vienen (Potosí 1576),

son aca muy ne̜çesaria y valen muy cara (New Granada 1577), sus
sobrina (Lima 1577), dezirme 'decidme' and salidas . . . tan
tardia (Panamá 1578), el rriego 'riesgo' que corren (Potosí 1580),
no e visto repuesta 'respuesta' (Lima 1581), repuesta 'respuesta'
(Mexico 1582), veged 'vejez' (Guatemala 1582), lo que (vos) ubierei
menester . . . (vos) no abei menester . . . (vos) podei pensar (Sto.
Domingo 1583), Chonin Blazque e Juan Sanchez (Panama 1583),
Montedoca 'Montesdoca' (Mexico City 1584), depues aca (twice)
'después acá' (Perú 1585), muchas tengo escrita (Mexico City 1587),
vos . . . no venites (Tunja 1587), sus benida (Cartagena 1590), pue
'pues' (Perú 1590), dos santissimo padres . . . hiernos y enparentado
. . . Catañeda 'Castañeda' (Mexico City 1590), desatre 'desastre'
(Sto. Domingo 1591), (tú) escrivite 'escribiste' (Panamá 1592), no
a abidos navíos (Plata 1593), (yo) os es (=he) embiado (Veracruz
1602), donde vos naciste 'naciste(i)s' (Mexico City 1602), vetro tio
(Lima 1604), and many more. Once again, the majority of examples
occur in letters from sevillanos.

8. Other letters from this period, mostly from sevillanos, yield:
me conose 'conocen' todos (Lima 1558), temgo verguemsa . . . em
españa . . . simquemta '50' (Lima 1559), no ebargante 'no embargante'
(Quito 1560), la voluntan . . . su voluntan . . . (Mexico City 1562),
puede . . . los honbres . . . anque sea mas buenos (Sto Domingo
1583), the hypercorrections aprienten 'aprieten' (Mexico City 1564),
lenjos 'lejos' (Popayán 1578), planta 'plata' (Mexico 1582), benten y
cinco (Venezuela 1584), distrinto 'distrito' (Lima 1586), al estante
'al instante' (Lima 1587), co mi contento . . . yo escribiren
'escribiré', agilaldo 'aguinaldo' (Panama 1587), aconmodada (Veracruz 1589), e ('en') mi conpañia (Cartagena 1590), admiranme lo
que dizen (Lima 1590), bie 'bien' (Perú 1590), pensadumbres (Cuzco
1590), los desatres (sic) que . . . a venido (Sto. Domingo 1591),
quatro dias que nos queda (Honduras 1599). However, muncho
'mucho', very popular in the 16th Century and still frequent today in
the substandard speech of both Spain and Spanish America, is not a
case of hypercorrection but acquired its syllable-final nasal by close
association with cuanto and tanto. (Compare Portuguese muito
where a nasal vowel has become standardized in speech (though
not in spelling) by analogy with /kwánto/ and /tánto/.)

9. Examples from other regions: mi hermana Beatriz e (=de)
Barrasa (twice) (Panamá 1559), to lo que 'todo lo que' (Zacatecas
1573), arcauz 'arcabuz' and da 'daga' (Mexico City 1575), calsaos
'calzados' (Lima 1583), proze 'procede' (Venezuela 1584), a to sus
hijas (Lima 1590), tan desea 'deseada' (Panamá 1592), de proho'
de provecho' (Guatemala 1600), Palo 'Pablo' (Guatemala 1600),
Xesucristo . . . lo ie 'guíe' de su mano (Guatemala 1600), no se si

pore escrivir 'podré', que yo consia 'consiga' (both Mexico City 1617), San Hosed 'San José', (N. Vizcaya 1635). (Loss of word final /d/, both in imperatives like vení, traé, decí, rogá, and in nouns like mitá, salú, mercé, is too well known to be worth mentioning.)

10. Biographical data (including birthplace) on over 55, 000 16th Century emigrants to the New World show that the Antilles and coastal areas of the Caribbean from the very beginning boasted a higher per-centage of Andalusian colonists than any other region of America: almost 50 percent. For the statistical breakdown by birthplace, year, and destination in America see Boyd-Bowman, Peter, Indice geobiográfico de 40, 000 pobladores españoles de América en el siglo XVI, Vols. I (1493-1519) and II (1520-1539), Bogotá, Instituto Caro y Cuervo, 1964, and Editorial Ius, México, D. F., 1968. Also, by the same author, 'La procedencia de los españoles de América: 1540-1559' in Historia Mexicana, XVII, 1967, 37-71, and Patterns of Spanish Emigration to the New World (1493-1580), Council on International Studies, SUNY at Buffalo, Special Studies No. 34 (1973), 97 pp. Still unpublished statistics on over 9, 500 colonists of known birthplace who emigrated between 1580 and 1600 brings my total to slightly over 55, 000 for the 16th Century as a whole.

11. For a discussion of Seville as the hub of Spain's maritime empire in the New World and the probable role of sailors and mer-chants in spreading Andalusian linguistic traits among the lowland coastal areas of the Caribbean and adjacent shores of the Pacific, see Boyd-Bowman (1956) 'Regional Origins of the Earliest Spanish Colonists of America', Publications of the Modern Language Associ-ation, 1152-1163, and Ramón Menéndez Pidal (1957) 'Sevilla frente a Madrid', in A André Martinet, Estructuralismo e historia, Catalán Menéndez Pidal, Diego, Ed., Canarias, Universidad de La Laguna, 00 165).

For a detailed study of early Spanish American phonology and an extensive bibliography of the subject, see Cline, William J., 1972, 'The Phonology of Sixteenth Century American Spanish', unpublished Ph. D. dissertation, State University of New York at Buffalo. This dissertation is one of many that has made or is making extensive use of Boyd-Bowman's computer-assisted data bank (LASCODOCS: Lin-guistic Analysis of Spanish Colonial Documents) in which linguistic phenomena of all kinds have been abundantly recorded and classified.

For a rich source of linguistic data, not merely lexical but also morphological and phonological, see Boyd-Bowman, Peter M., 1971, Léxico hispanoamericano del siglo XVI, London, Tamesis, 1004 pp.

IS OLD SPANISH A NODE ON THE STAMMBAUM?

WILLIAM J. CALVANO

Temple University

In his <u>Manual de gramática histórica española</u>, Ramón Menéndez Pidal characterizes Modern Spanish as a reflex of Vulgar Latin that has passed through a stage called Old Spanish. He defends Vulgar and not Classical Latin as the source of all the Romance Languages: 'Todas estas lenguas son una continuación moderna del latín vulgar hablado, sin preocupación literaria . . .' He further specifies that Vulgar Latin is not a reflex of Classical Latin, but is, rather, a coexisting system: 'El latín vulgar no se diferencia del clásico por la fecha, pues es tan antiguo, y más, que el latín literario; vivió siempre al lado de él, aunque no siempre divorciado de él.' Furthermore, Menéndez Pidal argues that our principal source for Vulgar Latin lies in its linguistic reconstruction: '. . . la ciencia se tiene que valer, principalmente, de la restitución hipotética de las formas vulgares, por medio de la comparación de los idiomas neolatinos. . . .'

It remained for Hall (1950) to clearly defend and rigorously apply the methodology of internal and external reconstruction of the ancestral form of the Romance languages. Hall advises us to reconstruct using first the most closely related languages to insure establishing correct intermediate stages. He cautions that close relation means that the languages share linguistic features or are bounded by the same isoglosses, not necessarily their geographical proximity.

Hall posits a 'stammbaum' or branching tree family relationship for the Romance languages. Proto-Romance is the ancestral form of all the Romance languages. It split into Proto-Southern and Proto-Continental. In turn, Proto-Continental split into Proto-Eastern and Proto-Italo-Western-Romance, the latter being what Menéndez

Pidal and others called Vulgar Latin. The other language states which Hall posits leading from Proto-Italo-Western-Romance to the Spanish branch are: Proto-Western, Proto-Ibero, and Northern-Ibero. Each node (or Proto-language) on the tree represents an intermediate language posited for structural reasons. Hall states that his proposed stammbaum is sketchy and tentative, and calls for its further elaboration. It is in this light that we ask: Is Old Spanish or Old Castilian an intermediate language stage, or node, on the Spanish historical family tree?

One area left unspecified by Hall is the determination of criteria for deciding whether linguistic systems are closely related and should therefore be grouped together on a node. It can be argued that mutual intelligibility is a weak criterion for measuring relatedness, since it lacks scientific precision and relies heavily on the intuition and linguistic capability of individuals. An interesting case where the mutual intelligibility criterion fails is cited by Saltarelli (1966). In this article, he compares the dialect of Pescaseroli, Italy, with Standard Italian. He points out that even though there is no difference in the vowel inventory of the two dialects, speakers of Standard Italian find the Pescaseroli dialect unintelligible. He attributes this fact to the morphophonemic system of the Pescaseroli dialect, the vowels of which undergo raising under certain circumstances and reduction to schwa under others.

Saltarelli's alternative is to determine the recurring set of formal properties, and to label them the Common System. The dialect differences are then generated as Extensional Systems. He is admittedly searching for a '. . . universal characterization of relatedness, distance, class membership, intelligibility, and other contrastively relevant concepts'. However, although his system considers relatedness, it has no criterion for measuring what degree of relatedness makes dialects one or two languages. Some sort of addition is needed to account for the fact that even though Castilian and Sardinian have five-vowel systems and Portuguese has a seven-vowel system, Castilian and Portuguese are structurally more closely related to each other than is either to Sardinian. In addition to their common phonemic stock, all three have a large corpus of cognate lexical items, and the distribution of the vowel phonemes in cognate lexical items is in a predictable relationship between Spanish and Portuguese, but not between Spanish and Sardinian nor between Portuguese and Sardinian. Therefore, it can be concluded that the presence of cognate items and the regular correspondence of phonemes in these items constitute good criteria for judging relative relatedness.

The scheme set forth by Agard (1970) requires that two or more dialects are to be classified as members of the same language or different languages for structural reasons. Structural similarity requires that they share a sufficiently large number of cognates of phonetically and semantically similar morphemes in regular phonological and grammatical correspondence. Regular phonological correspondence means that the cognate lexical items must be 'representable uniformly with a set of morphophones, not exceeding in size the inventory required to represent either one of them singly.'

The reasoning behind these postulates seems simple and sound. Given two systems which share the exact phonological structure but have no cognates and have different grammatical systems, they could hardly be called dialects of the same language. Agard cites Spanish and Basque or Russian and Mordvin, which are said to share phonemic inventories, as falling into this case.

At the other extreme are two systems which have similar grammatical systems, a large corpus of cognate lexical items, a stock of morphophones in regular though not predictable correspondence; this is the situation on which the theories of linguistic reconstruction are based. The relationship between Spanish and Sardinian and between Portuguese and Sardinian fit this category.

The third case, which falls between the two just cited, occurs when, in addition to grammatical similarity, the two dialects show cognate items which have a phonological structure in a predictable relationship. In searching for classificatory criteria for differentiation of the two sets of circumstances, it seems most reasonable to classify the unpredictable although reconstructable relationship as languages related to each other on the same family tree, while those so closely related that their structures are directly predictable should be classified as dialects of the same language.

Standard Madrid Spanish and Standard Latin American Spanish are in a predictable relationship even though the Madrid variety has two segments (/θ/ and /ř/. Predictability is unidirectional from Madrid to Latin American (/θ/ becomes /s/ and /ř/ becomes /y/), and they are dialects of the same language.

A similar unidirectional system of prediction exists between the Sicilian dialects of Palermo and Catania, both of which have the identical number and type of phonological units, but with differences in their distribution in cognate forms. In one type, a series of items shows /y/ or /r/ followed by a consonant in the Palermo dialect corresponding to a geminate consonant in the Catania dialect:

Palermo:	/kóypu	kóyti	várba	póyta/
Catania:	/kóppu	kótti	vávva	pótta/

The Catania form is always predictable from the Palermo form, but the converse is not true since there is another set of cognates which shows a geminate in both dialects (/fáttu/ in both beside /póyta,

pótta/), and this prevents the prediction from Catanese to Palermitano.
Their predictable relationship enables them to be classified as dialects of the same language which we shall call Sicilian.

Sicilian has the classical five-vowel system corresponding to a
seven-vowel system in Standard Italian and in a host of southern dialects on the peninsula. Both vocalic and consonantal systems of all
these dialects are in a predictable relationship; they are, therefore,
classified as members of the same language which we shall call
Italian. Sardinian is not a member of this group because of vowel
correspondences. The vocalic status of Sicilian vis à vis Sardinian
is considered apart to reinforce a point that will be made subsequently.

Even though Sicilian and Sardinian both have a five-vowel system,
there is a lack of predictability between them similar to the one cited
between Spanish and Sardinian. In Sardinian, /é/ corresponds sometimes to /é/ in Sicilian (/anéddu/ in both) and sometimes to /í/
(Sardinian /kéra/, Sicilian /číra/) with corresponding similarity in
the back vowels. The historical implications of this fact are of considerable importance.

Hall groups Sardinian, Lucanian, and Sicilian as descendents of
Proto-Southern-Romance. Standard Italian and other Italian dialects
come from Proto-Continental-Romance. These two, Proto-Southern
and Proto-Continental, have Proto-Romance as their immediate historical antecedent. Hall's hypothesis was tested by Mazzola (1967),
who said:

> It is proposed here that Sicilian lies every bit as much outside
> the domain of Italian linguistics as does Sard--as Hall rightly
> indicates, but for different reasons, in his 1950 article.
> Sicilian is clearly not an Italian dialect as has been generally
> assumed . . . but rather constitutes a separate language,
> distinct at first along with Sard from Italian and now distinct
> from Sard.

It is clear that Mazzola is not using the term 'language' in the
same sense that it is being used in this study. Instead, Mazzola
cites a list of consonantal changes which Sardinian and Sicilian share
with each other but which neither shares with Italian. However, none
of these changes affects the predictability between Sicilian and Italian,
and hence the language classification as proposed here requires that
Sicilian and the other Italian dialects be grouped together to the exclusion of Sardinian. Therefore, the historical relationship must be
reinterpreted, and Sicilian must be grouped along with the Italian
dialects.

Agard explains what sort of change affects the relationship, and
causes two different dialects to be classified as different languages:

What . . . is the mechanism by which an antecedent language
with two dialects 'splits' into two descendent languages? It
is to be seen as a process of partially intersecting merger,
such that the morphophones required for each descendent language are reduced to the same stock. The mergers must
intersect only partially, because if the two dialects share the
same (i. e. a totally intersecting) merger, there is no effect:
the two are still unified despite the lost morphophone. . . .
But the mergers must be intersecting and not independent,
because if one dialect merges somewhere in the vocalism
(say) while the other merges somewhere in the consonantism,
the two are still unifiable by taking into account both pre-
merger situations. . . . Thus from the moment two intersecting mergers have been completed--with identical reduction
of the stock--one language has become two. . . .

Agard explains further, in a footnote, that 'Splits do not enter in,
for the new morphophones are of course required by the dialects that
generate them, and hence globally.'

What, then, is the language relationship between contemporary
Spanish, Portuguese, and Judaeo Spanish? Are they one language or
more than one? We begin with a consideration of Spanish and Portuguese. Their morphophone vowel systems are identical if we use
/è/ and /ò/ to account for Spanish diphthongization. At first glance
the differences in their stocks of consonantal segments appear to be
minimal. In addition to the segments which they share in regular
correspondence, Spanish has /θ/ which Portuguese does not have,
and Portuguese has /v, š, ž, and z/ which Spanish does not have.
Portuguese (P) /s/ and /z/ both correspond sometimes to Spanish
(S) /θ/ and sometimes to /s/ (P /káza/ S /kása/, P /vézeš/ S
/béθes/, P /pásu/ S /páso/, P /sínku/ S /θínko/). Predictability of
these segments is impossible, and they must be classified as dialects of different languages.

In cognate lexical items, Castilian Spanish and Judaeo Spanish
share precisely the same vowel inventory and most of the same consonantal segments. Castilian alone has /θ/ and /ř/, and Judaeo
Spanish alone has /v, z, š, ž/. Castilian /ř/ converts very nicely
into Judaeo Spanish /y/ (/kabářo-kaváyo/), but Castilian /θ/ corresponds to /s/ in one series of correspondants in Judaeo Spanish
(/θínko/-/sínko/) and to /z/ in another series (/béθes/-/vézes/).
Since Judaeo Spanish /z/ also corresponds to Castilian /s/ in another set (/káza/-/kása/), predictability is impossible without reconstructing other segments; Castilian and Judaeo Spanish are dialects of two different languages.

From the data presented, Portuguese and Judaeo Spanish have a striking resemblance with regard to the fricative correspondences. Neither Judaeo Spanish nor Portuguese has the segment /θ/, and both have /s, z, š, ž/ in exact or predictable correspondence. The striking difference between the two is the nasal and lateral correspondences, but they, too, are in a predictable relationship. It would appear that in spite of a very complex conversion system, Judaeo Spanish and Portuguese could be considered dialects of the same language.

Daniel P. Dato (1959) presents a reconstruction of Proto-Ibero-Romance and a downtracing from Proto-Romance to Proto-Ibero-Romance through the intermediate stages of Proto-Continental, Proto-Italo-Western, and Proto-Western. Of course, this coincides exactly with Hall's stammbaum discussed earlier. Dato then continues his downtracing by splitting Proto-Ibero into Proto-East-Ibero and Proto-West-Ibero. The latter is the source of Galician and Portuguese, while Proto-East-Ibero splits into Asturian, Aragonese, and Proto-Spanish. In turn, Proto-Spanish splits into Judaeo-Spanish and Proto-Castilian, and the latter splits into Andalusian and Castilian. The latter part of Dato's family tree differs from Hall's split of Proto-Ibero into South-Ibero, which develops into Mozarabic, and North-Ibero which splits into Portuguese, Spanish, and Catalan. We shall take a somewhat detailed look at the structural changes which Dato posits for his classification in the light of the language theory under discussion. As a first consideration, at the bottom of Dato's tree is the split of Proto-Spanish into Castilian and Andalusian.

The chief distinction that Dato presents between Andalusian and Castilian is that the latter has a phonological contrast (/θ/=/s/) which the former does not have. Obviously, the relationship is predictable from the Castilian form. Castilian /θ/ converts directly to Andalusian /s/ (/péθes/ becomes /péscs/). The Andalusian /s/ is interdental in the ceceante dialects (/péθeθ/), and it is alveolar (/péses/) in the seseante dialects. A slightly more complicating circumstance is presented by those Andalusian dialects showing some sort of aspirate (whether bilabial or glottal) in initial position of words such as /hórno/. The problem can be circumvented by having all Andalusian /h/'s go to zero in Castilian (thus the initial /h/ of /hasér/ is deleted) and then Castilian /x/ converts to Andalusian /h/ (/áxo/ becomes /áho/). So, because of their predictable relationship, Andalusian and Castilian are to be classified as one language (Spanish, instead of Dato's Proto-Castilian).

Turning to the other end of Dato's stammbaum, Proto-Ibero-Romance is split into Proto-East-Ibero and Proto-West-Ibero. Proto-West-Ibero results from: (1) the change of initial voiceless stop plus /l/ to the voiceless sibilant /š/ (/plóra/ becomes /šóra/ and /kláma/

becomes /šáma/), (2) the reduction of the medial sequence /-men-/ in post tonic position to /-mV-/ (/nómene/ becomes /nómi/), (3) the insertion of a yod before the sequence /ša/ (/bášu/ becomes /bayšu/), (4) the change of /z/ to /ž/ in post yod position (/kéyzu/ becomes /kéyžu/), and (5) the loss of /D/ (/súDa/ becomes /súa/). The changes numbered (1) through (4) do not affect the predictable relationship between Proto-East-Ibero and Proto-West-Ibero. Change number (5) does, and we shall return to it later.

Proto-East-Ibero is the result of the following innovations: (1) the diphthongization of stressed lax mid vowels which are not in pre-palatal position (/cèlu/ becomes /cyèlu/ and /pòrta/ becomes /puèrta/), (2) the merger of /c/ and /ʒ/ to /c/ (/dɨʒes/ becomes /dɨces/ while /pócu/ remains the same), (3) the merger of /s/ and /z/ to /s/ (/káza/ becomes /kása/ while /pásu/ remains unchanged), (4) the merger of /ž/ and /š/ to /š/ (/žɔgu/ becomes /šwègu/ but /déša/ does not change), (5) the palatalization and reduction of the geminate /nn/ to /ñ/ (/ánnu/ becomes /áñu/), (6) the loss of yod in word final position and in syllable final position before any consonant except /t/ (/daréy/ becomes /daré/ and séypa/ becomes /sépa/), (7) the loss of /w/ in syllable final position (/ówtru/ becomes /ótru/), (8) the loss of /b/ after /m/ (/lómbu/ becomes /lómu/), (9) the restructuring of the medial sequence /-men-/ to /-mbr-/ (/ómene/ becomes /ómbre/), and (10) the merger of /D/ with /d/, (/súDa/ becomes /súda/).

Of the ten changes listed, only those which deal with the restructuring of the fricative systems and the loss of /D/ in conjunction with parallel though different changes for the same segments in Proto-West-Ibero result in a partially intersecting merger causing the resultant systems to be in an unpredictable relationship. Dato's split of Proto-Ibero-Romance into Proto-West-Ibero and Proto-East-Ibero is well motivated for the partially intersecting mergers of the segments /c, z, s, z/ and similarly of /D/ with /d/. In West-Ibero, /c/ and /s/ merge, as do /ʒ/ and /z/. In East-Ibero, /c/ and /ʒ/ merge, and so do /s/ and /z/. The resultant correspondences (/káza, kása/ but /vézes, veces/) illustrate the role of one partially intersecting merger, while the form /múda/ in both West-Ibero and East-Ibero in relationship to /súda/ in East-Ibero but /súa/ in West Ibero exemplifies the role of the loss of /D/ as another partially intersecting merger. Later, I shall consider these same partially intersecting mergers in conjunction with Judaeo-Spanish, but for the moment I continue with the downtracing.

Dato next separates Proto-East-Ibero-Romance into Proto-Spanish as one branch, and Aragonese and Asturian as the other branches. He notes that Aragonese and Asturian share some structural features, e.g. the diphthongization of /è/ and /ò/ even before palatals, but he also notes that Aragonese and Asturian show dissimilar development for other changes. For example, Proto-Ibero /ʎ/ remains in Aragonese, but becomes yod in Asturian. Aragonese retains the Proto-East-Ibero clusters /pl, Npl, kl, and yod t/ and Aragonese merges Proto-East-Ibero final /-u/ and /-o/. On the other hand, Asturian merges Proto-East-Ibero initial /l/ and medial geminate /-ll-/ as /c/, but it still distinguishes final /-u/ from final /-o/.

In Dato's words:

> The developments just described show some structural features which are similar in Aragonese and Asturian, while others indicate a contrast between the two. Therefore, in the absence of a stronger argument which would justify grouping Aragonese and Asturian together, it is best assumed that a three-way split took place in Proto-East-Ibero Romance separating Proto-Spanish from the two remaining reconstruction dialects.

I could add here that there are other partial similarities among the various dialects. For example, Portuguese and Asturian retain /ʎ/, and Portuguese and Aragonese retain the yod /t/ cluster.

In addition to Aragonese and Asturian, Dato splits Proto-Spanish from Proto-East-Ibero. The latter split is based on the following structural changes: (1) the complete loss of the phonemic contrasts /è/ with /é/ and /ò/ with /ó/ (Proto-East-Ibero /byènto/ becomes Proto-Spanish /byénto/ and /òy/ becomes /óy/), (2) the merger of /ʎ/ and /š/ to /š/ (/òʎu/ becomes /óšu/), (3) Proto-East-Ibero initial /pl/, /kl/ become /ʎ/ (/plánu/ becomes /ʎánu/), (4) geminate /-ll-/ changes to /ʎ/ (/bálle/ becomes /báʎe/), (5) Proto-Spanish merges the clusters yod /t/ and /Nʎ/ to /č/ (/múytu/ becomes /múčo/ and /inʎáre/ becomes /inčár/), (6) the loss in Proto-Spanish of initial /f/ (/féyto/ becomes /éčo/), (7) the raising of Proto-East-Ibero /ó/ to /í/ when it follows a yod and precedes a palatal (/syéʎa/ becomes /síʎa/, (8) the loss of final unstressed /e/ after /r/ (/kantáre/ becomes /kantár/), (9) the merger of word-final /-u/ and /-o/ to /-o/ (/gátu/ becomes /gáto/ while /súdo/ remains unchanged), and (10) the metathesis of Proto-East-Ibero /-rn-/ to /-nr/ (/tyénru/ becomes /tyérno/). Since no case of partially intersecting merger is cited, one must conclude that there is no motivation for the split of Proto-East-Ibero into Proto-Spanish, Asturian, and Aragonese. They are all dialects of the same language. With this in mind, I continue with Dato's downtracing from Proto-Spanish to Castilian.

It is at this point that Dato introduces Judaeo-Spanish and revises the downtracing from Proto-Ibero to Proto-East-Ibero. As I have already shown, Judaeo-Spanish shows the same development as

Portuguese with regard to the segments /c, ʒ, s, z/ and one must keep in mind that the different developments of these consonants led to the partially intersecting mergers which were a main reason for separating Proto-East-Ibero from Proto-West-Ibero. In Dato's presentation, Judaeo-Spanish and Castilian both develop from Proto-Spanish. Castilian comes from: (1) the merger of /v/ and /b/ (/ʈáve/ becomes /ʈábe), (2) the merger of /c/ and /ʒ/ to /c/ (/řaʒón/ becomes /řacón/, but /bráco/ remains the same), (3) the merger of /z/ and /s/ (/mezúra/ becomes /mesúra/, while /cesár/ remains the same), (4) the merger of /ž/ and /š/ to /š/ (/ližéro/ becomes /lišéro/, while /déša/ remains unchanged).

Judaeo-Spanish comes from Proto-Spanish as a result of the following changes: (1) the merger of /s/ and /c/ (/cínko/ becomes /sínko/, while /pása/ remains the same), (2) the merger of /ʒ/ and /z/ (/díʒen/ becomes /dízen/, while /káza/ remains the same), (3) the merger of /ʈ/ with yod (/ʈave/ becomes /yáve/, while /yá/ remains unchanged), and (4) the partial merger of /b/ and /v/.

Dato has grouped Judaeo-Spanish with Castilian with no mention of an alternative grouping, namely, the split of Proto-Ibero-Romance into those dialects which merge /ʒ/ with /z/ and /c/ with /s/ (Portuguese, Judaeo-Spanish, and Galician), and those which merge /c/ with /ʒ/ and /s/ with /z/ (Castilian). The status of Asturian and Aragonese remains unclear in this regard.

Neither analysis excludes the other, and both account for the data. However, after the introduction of Judaeo-Spanish in Dato's analysis, his separation of Proto-East-Ibero and Proto-West-Ibero rests on the development of phoneme /D/, which may be considered a somewhat weak criterion. It is true that, synchronically, the correspondences which lead to the reconstruction of /D/ would separate Portuguese from Judaeo Spanish in absolute terms of the reconstruction. However, the linguist using the predictability criterion faces similar decisions to those faced by the historical linguist, for example, dialect borrowing. Many times when reconstructing, certain items must be excluded from the reconstruction corpus because the correspondence shows an irregularity. Often, the irregularity can be explained in terms of borrowing (for example, the Spanish initial /pl/ cluster in /pláθa/ in view of /ʈáma, ʈéga/ etc.). Similarly, there are vocabulary items which synchronically present problems. In the Judaeo-Spanish of Salonica, Cynthia Crews (1935) records the form /dečidyó/ which she identifies as an italianate form because of the /č/ corresponding to /θ/ in Castilian (/deθidyó/). It is therefore excluded from the corpus of cognates in the synchronic relationship. Furthermore, it would seem reasonable that for those forms in which Portuguese and Judaeo-Spanish do not agree with regard to the /d/ correspondences, one set might be excluded as possible dialect borrowings. The sibilant correspondences, on the other hand, are too frequent and too regular to be considered exceptions. One must also keep in mind that the sibilant correspondences entail different segments rather than different distributions. This gives one small thread of motivation to the analysis which splits Proto-East-Ibero and Proto-West-Ibero on the grounds of the sibilant correspondences. Judaeo-Spanish then becomes a form of Proto-West-Ibero Romance.

A preliminary look at Catalan indicates that: (1) it shares the Portuguese seven-vowel system, (2) it resembles Aragonese in the conservation of initial /pl/, /fl/ and /kl/ (/pléna/, /fláma/ and /kláma/), and (3) it corresponds with Portuguese and Judaeo-Spanish in its contrast and distribution in cognate items of /s/ and /z/, with no /θ/ (/káza, pásus, sínk, Tansa, róza/). There is a strong probability that all the data will bring Catalan into Proto-Ibero-Romance. In that case, the merger of the medial sibilants will leave it in a predictable relationship with Portuguese and Judaeo-Spanish. Rather than using Dato's West-Ibero label, this language should perhaps be called Peripheral-Ibero.

It should be noted that since no systematic comparison of Ibero-Romance with Proto-Gallo-Romance is made here, no claim is made for their relationship, and more specifically, for the relationship between Provençal and Catalan. Furthermore, a detailed comparison of Ibero, Gallo, Italo, and other Romance groups using the predictability classification to judge membership in a language may, indeed, present a radically different stammbaum for the Romance Languages from the one presented by Hall and cited earlier.

It is time now to turn to 'Old Spanish' vis à vis Proto-Ibero, Peripheral-Ibero, contemporary Spanish, contemporary Portuguese, and contemporary Judaeo Spanish. Old Spanish, or Old Castilian, is cited with considerable frequency in the classical texts of historical Spanish or Romance, usually for a particular lexical item displaying some semantic or phonological peculiarity. Menéndez Pidal (1904) offers a sort of linguistic description of Old Spanish by listing its orthographic differences from modern Spanish usage. He gives enough description of the related phonetic structure for us to be able to abstract a linguistic description. His list of segments in Old Spanish includes: (1) the voiced and voiceless spirants /s/ and /z/ (/pasár/ /káza/), (2) the voiced and voiceless palatal affricates /c/ and /ʒ/ (/pláca/ /hazér/), (3) the voiced and voiceless palatal fricatives /š/ and /ž/ (/díše/ /kožér/), (4) the labio-dental voiced fricative /v/ (/áve/), and (5) the voiceless velar spirant /h/ (/hazér/). To this stock are presumably added the consonantal segments /p t č k b d g f m n ñ l ɾ/, but not /θ/ since, in his discussion of /c/ and /ʒ/, Menéndez Pidal explains that /θ/ is the contemporary result of their merger. The vowel system, one must assume, was identical with

present-day Spanish. Both with regard to the cluster yod /t/ instead
of /č/ and with the systematic status of open mid vowels, some argument could be offered but is here ignored, for such argument does not
affect the language classification of Old Spanish. The presence of the
sibilants which must be reconstructed /c ẓ s z/, and its overall similarity to Dato's reconstructed parent language point to its status as
Proto-Ibero-Romance. Whatever peculiarities it has could be considered dialect variations within the language system; its status as
the dialect from which contemporary Spanish developed is not contradicted. However, Old Spanish is not a separate node on the family
tree.

REFERENCES

Agard, F. B. 1970. Language and dialect: Some tentative postu-
    lates. Linguistics.
Crews, Cynthia. 1935. Recherches sur le judéo-espagnol dans les
    Pays Balkaniques. Paris.
Dato, Daniel P. 1959. A historical phonology of Castilian. Un-
    published doctoral dissertation, Cornell University.
Hall, Robert A., Jr. 1950. The reconstruction of Proto-Romance.
    Lg. 26.6-27.
Mazzola, Michael L. 1967. The place of Sicilian in the reconstruc-
    tion of Proto-Romance. Unpublished doctoral dissertation, Cor-
    nell University.
Menéndez Pidal, Ramón. 1904. Manual de gramática histórica
    española. Madrid, Espasa Galpe.
Saltarelli, Mario. 1966. Romance dialectology and generative
    grammar. Orbis.

EL HABLA DE LAS CLASES JÓVENES
EN PUERTO RICO:
PROYECCIONES HACIA UNA LENGUA FUTURA

MARCELINO CANINO-SALGADO

Universidad de Puerto Rico

La peculiar situación histórica, geográfica, política y cultural de
la Isla de Puerto Rico se ha proyectado siempre en la preocupación
por nuestros fenómenos lingüísticos: ¡prístino espejo donde se pre-
senta una dimensión de nuestra auténtica cultura!

Nadie sería capaz de negar que los espíritus más alertas de nuestro
país están sumamente preocupados por la suerte y derrotero que
seguirá el español hablado de la Isla, sobre todo, en medio de la
crisis espiritual, social y política por la cual atraviesa Puerto Rico.

Algunos intelectuales extranjeros, entre ellos, Dámaso Alonso,
creen que el español de Puerto Rico se convertirá en una especie de
papiamento. En el caso del citado filólogo y linguista español, su
preocupación se fundamenta en lo que yo denomino la fobia contra el
anglicismo. Declaraba el Sr. Alonso en marzo de 1969:

> En Puerto Rico el peligro del anglicismo es especialmente
> grave, puede romper la forma interior del lenguaje, y al cabo
> de algunos decenios separar el habla de la Isla, de la del
> conjunto hispánico, es decir, convertirla en una especie de
> papiamento. Sería lamentable. [1]

Pero ese alarmismo sobre el peligro de corrupción del español
hablado en Puerto Rico, no es cosa reciente. En el año de 1947, hace
ya 27 años, el notable poeta español don Pedro Salinas publicaba en
la prensa del país las expresiones siguientes:

. . . que la lengua está en un momento de peligro; que el mal
reside en la falta de una conciencia lingüística; que los puertorriqueños no sentimos bien 'todo lo que vale y significa el idioma
en la vida del individuo y de un pueblo'; que hemos perdido la
conciencia del estado actual del idioma; que la lengua aquí 'es
una invitación contínua a la confusión mental, al equívoco y a
la pobreza expresiva.'[2]

El motivo de la preocupación de Don Pedro Salinas en 1947, fue el
mismo que preocupó a Dámaso Alonso en 1969:   el haber leído y
escuchado en Puerto Rico multitud de palabras inglesas; en otras
palabras, una preocupación nacida de la 'anglofobia.'
    Y lo interesante del caso es, que, esta fobia contra el anglicismo
no sólo la expresan los españoles o puertorriqueños hispanófilos en la
Isla, sino que la misma actitud alarmante se encuentra entre los
intelectuales españoles respecto del español de España.
    En 1966 Salvador de Madariaga escribió lo siguiente en la Revista
de Occidente:

La lengua española va rápidamente a una situación humillante
de mera colonia del inglés bajo el efecto combinado de la
indiferencia de los cultos, la presión de las agencias anglo-
sajonas de información, el vigor de los periódicos en lengua
española de propiedad norteamericana y la pereza o incom-
petencia de los traductores de libros, prensa y sobre todo
cine.[3]

Y añade algo que me enfada terriblemente:

En Méjico (y no digamos en Puerto Rico) nuestro lenguaje
se está pudriendo. En el resto de Suramérica y aun en
España va por el mismo camino.[4]

Ahora bien, me pregunto yo: ¿Será que comienzan estos
señores a escuchar el preludio al canto de cisne de la lengua española?
    Don Rafael Lapesa explica la situación que preocupó a Salinas,
Alonso, y Madariaga, de forma muy sensata. Refiriéndose a la
situación lingüística de España, dice:

. . . desde hace tres siglos vamos a remolque del restante
mundo occidental, tanto en las innovaciones con que la ciencia
y la técnica han cambiado las condiciones de la vida humana,
cuanto en la exploración de nuevos derroteros para las ideas.
Primero fuimos a la zaga de Francia; después, a la de Francia,
Inglaterra y Alemania; ahora, además, a la de Estados Unidos.

Con las ideas y las cosas vienen inevitablemente las palabras.
Ante este hecho, las lamentaciones son tan inútiles como las
protestas. [5]

Y luego, con esa salud intelectual que le caracteriza, añade
Lapesa:

La única actitud positiva consistirá en aprovecharnos del im-
pulso ajeno tan habilmente que en un futuro más o menos
próximo podamos seguir nuestro camino con autonomía; y
por lo que se refiere al lenguaje, asimilar lo necesario para
que nuestro idioma se mantenga a la altura de los tiempos,
sin dejar de responder a lo que éstos exigen; pero evitar en
lo posible que tal puesta al día menoscabe su belleza y
peculiaridad. [6]

Lapesa reconoce aquí que la lengua tiene sus leyes internas y que
sus estructuras cambian según los requerimientos y anhelos de los
que la hablan, pero mantiene el prurito artístico y nacionalista:
evitar el menoscabo de 'su belleza y peculiaridad'. ¡Nada más
natural y justo!
Y a diferencia de los autores anteriormente citados, Lapesa no se
asusta tanto con el chorro o fracatán de anglicismos o barbarismos
que se introducen en el español; más bien explica el fenómeno.
Veamos:

El aluvión de extranjerismos no es problema que afecte solo
al español. Por todas partes se oyen clamores parecidos,
como ya dice Madariaga. Es que el mundo se nos queda chico.
Tenemos noticia inmediata de lo que está pasando en Los
Angeles, la Ciudad del Cabo, Nueva Delhi o Göteborg, y con
frecuencia lo vemos 'en directo.' La comunicación es tan
rápida que no deja tiempo a traducciones reposadas. Las
novedades técnicas--desde el ciclotrón al humilde rollito de
cinta adherente--se difunden a toda prisa con su nombre de
origen, antes que se le busque sustituto, y muchas veces sin
que quepa buscárselo por ser marca registrada. La
frecuencia de viajes, el intercambio de turistas, estudiosos
y emigrantes, todo conduce a la creciente uniformación de
horizontes y ambientes vitales, a la familiaridad con lo que
antes era extraño, a su infiltración en ideas, costumbres,
maneras y lenguaje. En un mundo en que se internacio-
nalizan sociedades masificadas el purismo lingüístico está
condenado al más rotundo fracaso. [7]

Y, don Rubén del Rosario, el distinguido lingüista puertorriqueño, en 1955, mucho antes que Lapesa, refiriéndose al anglicismo en el español de Puerto Rico, apuntaba:

En general, el anglicismo en Puerto Rico se tolera socialmente, se acepta como una necesidad expresiva del tiempo nuevo. Que ha habido una reacción castellanizadora en los últimos treinta años, eso es indudable, eso era esperable. También ha habido exceso por parte de los innovadores. Pero mientras subsistan las relaciones políticas y culturales con el mundo angloameri- cano, mientras sean ellos los que inventen cosas nuevas y nosotros los que las recibamos, mientras los pueblos hispánicos, prefieran la retórica a la creación científica, tendremos anglicismos. . . . Progresivamente más anglicismos. [8]

Veamos ahora, a vuelo de pájaro, la situación lingüística de Puerto Rico, en lo que se refiere al habla de las clases jóvenes en varios niveles socioculturales. Veamos también si en términos lingüísticos los anglicismos están haciendo estragos o corrompiendo el español de Puerto Rico. Aunque nuestras observaciones se limitan más bien a los jóvenes de ambos sexos de todos los niveles socio- culturales y económicos entre los 15 a los 35 años, a veces echamos mano a materiales o datos lingüísticos provenientes de personas mayores (35-50) siempre y cuando dichos datos sirvan para establecer comparaciones o corroborar hechos.

Origen del problema

Hace cerca de quince años los profesores universitarios y aun las personas de mediana cultura han venido observando cómo una especie de trunquedad o manquera expresiva ha ido caracterizando a los estudiantes de Escuela Superior y nivel universitario.

Dio testimonio del fenómeno aludido, el notable escritor puertorri- queño y profesor universitario Luis Rafael Sánchez en un artículo publicado en el periódico local Claridad que tituló La generación O Sea. [9]

Reproducía Sánchez en su artículo la respuesta que uno de sus estudiantes dió a una pregunta formulada por aquél:

O sea que el personaje se suicida a sí mismo con pastillas de dormir, o sea que el personaje se mata a sí mismo, o sea con una dosis grande de supositorios (por soporíferos).

Pero este ejemplo no es tan sorprendente como los que mi colega, el Dr. Eliezer Narváez y yo, hemos encontrado consuetudinariamente en nuestros cursos universitarios, ejemplos claros de interferencia lingüística. Ya no se trata de casos de solecismos ni de metátesis, ni de reducciones fonéticas o de la fosilización de dialectalismos morfológicos, sino de desplazamientos acentuales, calcos fonéticos, alteraciones acústicas y construcciones sintácticas innovadoras (no quiero decir anglicadas).

Pero lo sorprendente es que nuestros cursos se convierten casi en un monólogo interior del estudiante y en un soliloquio del catedrático. ¡No hay una efectiva comunicación!

La limitación léxica de los estudiantes les hace perder tiempo buscando en su hueco archivo de posibilidades expresivas lo que no tienen. En estos casos dicen: 'Es que lo tengo en la punta de la lengua, pero no lo sé decir como es, usted sabe no, o sea, es que . . .'

Y ahí sigue el 'no se qué que deja balbuciendo'.

Donde no ocupa espacio la palabra se coloca una sonrisa mediana o mediadora, se organiza una gesticulación trunca, se oscurece la sílaba última de la oración como advertencia de la limitación o mutilación expresiva . . .'[10]

La limitación cognoscitiva de un léxico apropiado, les hace crear un léxico de ambigüedades; jamás se denominan las cosas por su nombre exacto, sino a través de términos 'como el Deso, la Desa, el Coso, el Cosito, la Cosita, la Vaina Esa, el Simiñoco, el Aparatito que es como una cosita redondita.' Y no digamos de cuando suelen dar direcciones: 'Mire, usted coge, por aquí, derechito . . ., dobla pá' este lao, se mete por un cuesta que tiene tres palos a un lao, la primera casa no, ni la otra, una casa allí, grande, esa es.' Usted nunca llega al lugar.

La trunquedad expresiva y la limitación léxica de los estudiantes universitarios, la mayor parte de ellos provenientes de la clase media y media alta, se debe, en parte, a una especie de enajenación lingüística. Esa falta de creatividad y precisión en la comunicación oral de los mencionados grupos estudiantiles, puede deberse a diferentes factores, entre ellos:

(1) El hecho indiscutible de que en nuestros hogares se dialoga cada día menos.

(2) La profusión comercializada de medios de propaganda comunicativa que, con trampas psicológicas, se dirigen sólo a la vista y al oído, sin que sea necesario una respuesta 'verbal activa'. Esto convierte al Ser Humano que escucha en un ser pasivo y en autómata de consumo.

(3) La radio, el cine, la televisión, los métodos audiovisuales mal empleados, y otros medios mecánicos han conseguido,

paulatinamente, el anquilosamiento de nuestras facultades expresivas.

¿Niveles socio-lingüísticos?

Sin embargo, hemos observado, como a diferencia de la mayor parte de los estudiantes universitarios y jóvenes de la Clase Media, la 'gente del pueblo' de niveles socio-económicos y culturales más bajos que los de la Clase Media, de todas edades y sexos--y aún los analfabetos--poseen gran fluidez expresiva y sorprendente precisión en la conversación. Claro está que el chorro caudaloso de arcaísmos léxicos y morfosintácticos, así como dialectalismos morfológicos, palabras de libre creación, neologismos y anglicismos castellanizados, junto a modismos, refranes y frases idiomáticas están presentes en el acervo lingüístico de los estratos populares en Puerto Rico. Y aunque los puristas académicos levanten sus voces de protesta contra estas expresiones que ellos suelen llamar: 'idiotismos', 'barbarismos', 'corrupción lingüística' o 'mancillamiento de la lengua castiza de los españoles', no importa; para el pueblo lo importante es la comunicación plena entre sus semejantes.

Pero veamos de inmediato algunos de los modismos, frases hechas y anglicismos que enfadan a los académicos y puritanos señores de la hispanofilia puertorriqueña.

Entre los modismos puertorriqueños más conocidos y significativos cito los siguientes:

1. arrancarle a uno el brazo: aceptar una oferta inmediatamente.
2. botar la pelota: algo extraordinario.
3. caerse del coy: darse en la cabeza, ser bruto.
4. cambiársele a uno los cables: comportarse afeminadamente.
5. coger un buche: guardar silencio.
6. coger por el cuello: regañar, amonestar.
7. comer pavo: sufrir un desencanto.
8. comer banco: no ser considerada para nada en un lugar, aburrirse.
9. como mear y sacudir: cosa fácil de poca importancia.
10. como caballo en vega: con toda libertad.
11. como Pedro por su casa: con exceso de confianza.
12. correrle a uno la máquina: embromar a uno.
13. creer que mea champán y caga bizcocho: ser presumido u altanero.
14. chavar la paciencia: molestar, fastidiar.
15. darle de arroz y de masa: acometer furiosamente.
16. darle como a pillo de película: Ibid.
17. darle como a pándereta de aleluya: Ibid.

18. darle derecha a uno: ignorar, sacar el cuerpo.
19. darle a uno un fajazo: pedirle dinero a uno.
20. echárselas más que Kresto: ser muy presumido.
21. empaquetar a uno: engañar a alguien.
22. estar en el guiso: participar de beneficios sin muchos esfuerzo.
23. estar que corta: tener coraje, estar molesto.
24. estar pichándole a uno: obtener algo de uno mediante halagos.
25. estar más jalao que un timbre de guagua: estar débil.
26. hablar más que una lavandera sin tabaco: hablar excesivamente.
27. hacerse el chivo loco: ignorar, no prestar atención.
28. hacerse el sorrocloco: hacerse el desentendido.
29. joder la pita: fastidiar, molestar.
30. meterle a uno los mochos: intimidar, fastidiar.
31. morir como el pez: comer demasiado.
32. nacarile del Oriente: negación rotunda o enfática.
33. no decir ni ji: no hacer comentario alguno.
34. no llegar ni a primera: no alcanzar sus objetivos.
35. pegarle un vellón a uno: incitar a hablar de algo que agrada a una persona.
36. ponerle a uno una cascarita: provocar reacciones expontáneas y comprometedoras.
37. ponerle a uno la batola: controlar a uno, coartarle la libertad.
38. ponerse pico a pico: discutir acaloradamente.
39. ser un cholipelao: no tener cabellos en la cabeza, ser calvo.
40. ser una perla: ser truhán.
41. tener aceite en la lámpara: ser inteligente.
42. tener uno una cereta: estar embriagado, tener mucho pelo.
43. tener uno más golpes que un baile de bomba: tener contestaciones inmediatas y atinadas.
44. tener una rajita: tener sangre negra.
45. tener un berrinche: estar enojado.
46. tener un compinche: tramar algo en grupo furtivamente.
47. tener la cara pará: demostrar enfado.
48. tener el moño parao: demostrar enfado y presumir de autoritario.

Entre viejas frases y modismos usados en el habla cotidiana de Puerto Rico, se encuentran un gran número de frases y modismos de nueva factura.

A mi juicio, aunque muchas de estas frases empiezan a incorporarse al lenguaje oral, por la frecuencia en que suelen escucharse llevan ya la señal de que permanecerán o formarán parte del viejo acervo lingüístico nuestro. La mayor parte de estas frases hechas, provienen del inglés, pero sus fonemas se realizan según los hábitos articulatorios y psicológicos del español. Por eso empleo una grafía española en su transcripción. Veamos parte del repertorio:

1. bien isi: del inglés easy, cosa fácil, suave, delicada, con ternura.
2. cucar a uno: incitar a uno.
3. creerse o ser un mamito: presumir de guapo o lindo.
4. crucear a uno: mirar insistentemente a una persona de arriba a bajo.
5. darse uno un papaso: estirarse el pelo encaracolado.
6. echar pa' encima: acometer.
7. echar pa' un sitio: salir hacia un lugar.
8. estar en algo: dedicarse obstinadamente a un placer.
9. estar caliente: poseer alucinógenos o cosas robadas.
10. estar embalao: estar bajo efectos de drogas.
11. estar tripiando: Ibid.
12. estar en órbita: ponerse a tono con un grupo.
13. estar en la onda: Ibid.
14. estar friquiando: disfrutar la música con mariguana o bebidas embriagantes.
15. estar guillao: disimular algo.
16. estar tiltiao: estar sumamente embriagado o alucinado.
17. estar por el libro: estar bien vestido, ser agradable.
18. estar op: estar eufórico (del inglés up).
19. estar tostao: ver el número 10.
20. estar mosqueao: estar desanimado.
21. estar en el traqueteo: participar en algo.
22. fletear a uno: mirar a una persona obstinadamente con lascivia.
23. gufiar a uno: observar disimuladamente a alguien.
24. hacer el plante: conquistar a una chica.
25. hacer cráneo: crear un estado de ánimo.
26. hacer cachipa: tener relaciones con lesbianas.
27. hacer pritibodi: exhibirse presumiendo belleza. (de pretty-body).
28. inventar uno algo: buscar con qué entretenerse.
29. ¡inventando ahí . . . !: delata entretenimientos no de su gusto.
30. levantar a una: conquistar.
31. mangarse a uno: sacarle dinero.
32. meter mano: acometer, participar activamente.
33. romper uno: Ibid.
34. ser pana o panín: ser amigo íntimo.
35. ser güilson: ser buena persona; también: ser chévere.
36. ser entendido: conocer a los homosexuales disimulados.
37. ser un tipo clin: ser decente.
38. ser loca cafre: homosexual sin decoro o discreción.

39. sabérselas todas: tener mentalidad amplia, no escandalizarse.
40. tener uno un punto: alcanzar un grado de relajamiento con bebidas embriagantes o alucinógenos.
41. tener un daun: estar deprimido (del inglés down)
42. tener un guille: presumir de algo.
43. tirar bomba: dejar esperando a alguien, quedar mal en un compromiso.
44. tirar cañona: Ibid.

Las transferencias lingüísticas en el habla de las clases jóvenes en Puerto Rico. Las palabras se desgastan o desaparacen fundamentalmente dentro de la lengua popular tan expuesta a las modas y vacilaciones lingüísticas. Veamos:

1. Los estados de ánimo. Para aludir a los estados de ánimo emocionales y físicos, así como para referirse a condiciones y atributos humanos, nuestros jóvenes emplean variadísimas formas lingüísticas que resultan verdaderamente interesantes, aunque nuestro particular prurito de 'hombre culto' nos haga recibirlas con cierto recato:

Tener un daun (estar deprimido)
Estar craqueao (estar desajustado emocionalmente)
Estar mosqueao (estar despitado o asustado)
Ser un tipo clin (ser decente)
Ser un tipo gruby (ser agradable)
Estar por el libro (ser correcto)
Estar por la maceta (inmejorable)
Estar filete (inmejorable)
Ser un tipo güilson (ser decente)

Estas formas son las de mayor frecuencia de uso entre las 44 anteriormente transcritas.

2. El adverbio 'mucho'. En el habla popular, en todos los niveles y sobre todo dentro de los grupos jóvenes, el adverbio mucho se sustituye por las formas:

a montones (había queso a montones)
en cospe (dulces en cospe)
un reguerete (un reguerete de galletitas)
a montón (bizcocho a montón)
a pasto (estaba el licor a pasto)
a tutiplén (gente a tutiplén)

choreto (estaba el guineo choreto)
en bruto (había gente en bruto)
un fracatán (compré un fracatán de arroz)

3. Nuevos objetos. La aparición de nuevos objetos en la vida
doméstica, la incorporación a nuestro sistema de conceptos y
estructuras de procedencia anglosajona y, sobre todo, norteamericana, ha dado lugar a que adoptemos y adaptemos--a veces--palabras
inglesas:

ballpoint pen (bolígrafo)
folder (cartapacio)
paper clip (presilla)
staple (engrapadora)
closet (armario empotrado)
plug (clavija)
tape player (tocacintas)
vacuum cleaner (aspiradora de polvo)
clutch (embrague), (P.R. cloche)

Aunque poseemos palabras equivalentes españolas en el habla
popular de Puerto Rico, las formas que hemos copiado arriba se
emplean indistintamente y a veces se alternan con las formas
españolas.

Dentro de las clases culta y rural de Puerto Rico, y contraria-
mente a lo que se creía antes, hay una marcada tendencia a rechazar
las palabras de origen inglés. Testimonio de esto lo dan las investigaciones sobre dialectología puertorriqueña que se realizan en
el Departamento de Estudios Hispánicos de la Universidad de Puerto
Rico.

El problema lingüístico se complica, pues la escuela pretende
enseñar normas de corrección y un buen manejo del vernáculo, a
la vez que confunde la conciencia lingüística del estudiante con la
imposición de la lengua inglesa desde que éste acude a la escuela
primaria.

Por un lado se impone la enseñanza del inglés; por otro, se pretende conservar un español inmaculado. ¡No se logra ni una cosa
ni otra!

Conviene señalar que la interferencia de las lenguas española e
inglesa es un hecho real. Desde el punto de vista cultural y político
la interferencia del inglés en el español es mucho más peligrosa y
nociva que la del español puertorriqueño en el inglés.

En un interesante estudio la distinguida lingüista Rose Nash[11] ha
probado cómo el arraigado acento y entonación del español puertorriqueño es uno de los obstáculos mayores que impiden el aprendizaje

del inglés por parte de los jóvenes universitarios de Puerto Rico. Asimismo la profesora Lucrecia Casiano[12] halló que el inglés hablado por los puertorriqueños que viven en Nueva York está muy matizado por la entonación del español de Puerto Rico.

Nada extraño sería pensar que como gran parte de los jóvenes de estratos socio-económicos limitados, por diversas razones, se ven obligados a abandonar las escuelas públicas del país, logren de esta forma salvarse un poco de los estragos que causa imponer un bilingüísmo a la fuerza. Por otro lado, la cantidad de frases y palabras inglesas que aprenden con toda libertad de espíritu y sin que nadie les obligue, junto a los dialectismos morfológicos y la lengua que aprendieron desde niños en sus humildes hogares, ayuda a una efectiva comunicación humana. No olvidemos que es dentro de las clases populares donde menos prejuicios puristas hay; pero recordemos que estos grupos son los más expuestos a las modas, ¡y las modas, modas son!

No quiero terminar sin citar unas palabras del maestro Rubén del Rosario:

. . . en Puerto Rico, la convivencia del inglés y el español ha producido una serie de cambios en una y otra lengua y algunos desajustes. La forma actual de esa convivencia es objetable porque uno de los idiomas se ha impuesto por razones políticas y no por razones de cultura. Es también objetable que muchos puertorriqueños hayan sobreestimado la importancia del inglés.

Y añade:

Lo urgente hoy a mi juicio es crear una actitud de máxima tolerancia frente a las variaciones del lenguaje, sin agollamientos puristas, sin patriotería. La verdadera lengua de los puertorriqueños es la lengua oral, la lengua cotidiana. Esa es la que todos tenemos que prestigiar.[13]

El que suscribe--ha sido victima--como tantos jóvenes puertorriqueños, de la interferencia lingüística del inglés, aunque no por razones de cultura, sino por razones políticas y comerciales. Y el problema a mi modo de ver es que mientras perdure en Puerto Rico una educación que rehuya sus raíces autóctonas y se norteamericanice cada día más sin ton ni son, es decir, sin razon cultural alguna, más crecerá la enajenación lingüística en la Isla.

Recuerdo un chiste de un amigo que envió a su hijo a estudiar en una universidad norteamericana para que aprendiera inglés sin acento. Al cabo de un año el hijo escribió al padre: 'Papi, no aprendo inglés, olvido el español . . .' El padre contesto: 'Nene, vente para acá, antes que te quedes mudo . . .'

En realidad, no sabemos de ningún pueblo en la historia que se haya quedado mudo, ni de ningún otro que por prestigiar su lengua oral se haya desmoralizado.

Siempre pienso que cuando Cicerón tronaba contra los galos y celtas que llenaban de barbarísmos la lengua latina, no soñó con el esplendoroso futuro: de esos barbarismos nacieron el francés de Victor Hugo y el español de Cervantes. No estoy loco por tanto, si sueño con una futura lengua puertorriqueña. Eso lo determinará el tiempo, ¡sedimentador implacable de toda actividad humana!

NOTES

1. Brignoni, Bartolomé. Damaso Alonso dice anglicismo convertirá el español de Puerto Rico en papiamento. En: El Mundo, San Juan, Puerto, Rico, 31 de marzo de 1969, p. 10C.

2. Citado por Rosario, Ruben del. La crisis del lenguaje. En: El Mundo, San Juan, Puerto Rico, 16 de febrero de 1947.

3. Madariaga, Salvador. Vamos a Kahlahtahyood. En: Revista de Occidente, Madrid, marzo, 1966, No. 36, p. 365.

4. Ibid.

5. Lapesa, Rafael. Kahlahtahyood. Madariaga ha puesto el dedo en la llaga. En: Revista de Occidente, Madrid, marzo, 1966, No. 36, p. 373.

6. Ibid., p. 374.

7. Ibid.

8. Rosario, Rubén del. Localismo y arcaísmo. En: La lengua de Puerto Rico. Río Piedras, Ed. Cultural, 1970, p. 22.

9. Sánchez, Luis Rafael. La generación O Sea. En: Claridad, San Juan, Puerto Rico, 23, I, 1972, p. 22.

10. Ibid.

11. Nash, Rose. Intonational Interterference in the speech of Puerto Rican bilinguals. En: Journal of English as a Second Language, Vol. IV, No. 2, Fall, 1969, pp. 1-42.

12. Casiano Montañez, Lucrecia. La pronunciación de los puertorriqueños. Tesis para el M. A. en Estudios Hispánicos, Universidad de Puerto Rico, 1965, 102 p.

13. Rosario, Rubén del. Espíritu y lengua. En: La lengua de Puerto Rico. Río Piedras, Ed. Cultural, 1970, p. 28.

SPANISH GLIDES REVISITED

WILLIAM W. CRESSEY

Georgetown University

Spanish glides have been the subject of considerable controversy.[1]
Mainly, this discussion has centered around the correct representation of glides at the phonemic level (i. e. should glides be represented
phonemically as vowels, as consonants, or as glides?). However,
much of the disagreement in this area was due, as pointed out by
Harris (1969:26), to certain methodological constraints to which
autonomous phonemicists adhered without any apparent motivation.
Specifically, a large part of the problem was the failure to recognize
that phonetic glides may have more than one phonemic source (i. e.
they may be derived in some instances from vowels, in others from
consonants, and in still others from glide phonemes). In addition,
failure to recognize the possible effects of morpheme boundaries led
Bowen and Stockwell (1956) to base part of their argument on the
presence of 'open juncture'. According to Bowen and Stockwell, the
presence of 'open juncture' accounts for the appearance of a [y] consonant in words such as abyecto, inyección, and deshielo, whereas
words like desierto and abierto (without 'open juncture') have a glide
[j]. Thus, according to Bowen and Stockwell's argument, since 'open
juncture' accounts for the phonetic [y], the two segments ([y] and [j])
are not in phonemic contrast in these words. Although Bowen and
Stockwell's use of 'open juncture' is questionable, it is interesting to
note that in all cases where they need to postulate its presence, there
is a perfectly well-motivated morpheme boundary.

This paper will not seek to reopen the matter of the phonemic
status of glides, but rather to investigate certain characteristics of
the rule (or rather rules) which introduce glides into Spanish utterances. Briefly, the claim will be made that there are two glide

formation rules in Spanish--one marking convention which applies to
high vowels only, and only within words, and one variable rule which
applies potentially to any nonlow vowel, and which may apply across
word boundary.

First, it will be necessary to discuss and take a position on certain ambiguities regarding the 'phonetic' description of the segments
in question. Navarro Tomás (1968) postulates three types of reduction of vowel segments: vocales relajadas, semivocales, and semi-
consonantes. The environment given for the laxed vowels is in a
syllable between a main stress and a secondary stress (for example
the i̱ in each of the words in (1). The semivowels are those glides
which occur after the syllabic nucleus (the i̱'s in (2)) and the semiconsonants are those which occur before the syllabic nucleus (the
i̱'s in (3)).

	(1)		(2)		(3)
	púlpito		veinte		piedra
	retótica		baile		bien
	católico		paisaje		labio
	admirable		estoico		tierno

Navarro's presentation is somewhat confused by the fact that, in
the case of mid vowels, he uses the same symbol for the laxed vowel
and for the semivowel. Thus the words in (4a) are all transcribed
with [ọ], which represents laxed o̱ and those in (4b) are also transcribed with [ọ], which in these cases represents the back mid glide
derived from o̱. Navarro gives as his reason 'la conveniencia de no
complicar demasiado la transcripción'; therefore one should not conclude that he means to equate the lax vowels and the mid glides in
a strict phonetic sense.

	(4a)		(4b)	
	temporal		toalla	
	redomado		coagular	
	ignorancia		cohete	
	símbolo			
	época			

Harris (1970:131) points out the difficulty of making accurate
phonetic assessments of these phenomena which only occur in relatively fast speech, and does make the assumption, consistent with
Navarro's notation, that there is 'no difference between a very short
vowel and a glide'.

Stockwell and Bowen (1965), on the other hand, do make a distinction between shortening and reduction to semivowel. They point out
that the phrases in (5a) have at least two pronunciations each: one
involving a laxed (or 'shortened', in their terminology) vowel (e.g.

[si εsta]), and the other involving a glide (e.g. [sjεsta]). However, each of the single words in (5b) has only the second pronunciation (the one with the glide). For this reason, this paper will take the point of view that there are two different segment types: laxed (or shortened) vowels (which are [+syllabic, -tense]), and glides (which are [-syllabic, -tense]).

On the other hand, the distinction drawn by Navarro Tomás between semivowels and semiconsonants will not be maintained, but rather the articulatory and acoustic differences between these two types of segments will be considered an automatic physiological consequence of the surrounding segments.[2] A glide, then, for the purposes of this paper, is any nonsyllabic reduction of a vowel, which occurs either before or after the syllabic nucleus. There are high and mid glides, but there are no low glides.

The foregoing phonetic discussion is presented in the spirit of resolving the phonetic ambiguities in one way or another, in order to be able to formulate the rules which I wish to discuss, and although I feel that I have good reasons for resolving them in the ways that I have, I do not think the argumentation to be presented would be contradicted by choosing to answer the phonetic questions differently.

(5a)	si esta	(5b)	siesta
	mi asma		miasma
	que asma		quiasma
	que hosco		quiosco

I turn now to the question of glide formation rules and their formulation.

Harris (1969:31, 122-123) argues that some phonetic glides must be represented as glides at the systematic phonemic level. He cites two sorts of data to support this contention.

(1) Verbs such as cambiar are conjugated with stem final glides ([kámbjo], etc.) whereas verbs such as ampliar are conjugated with stem final stressed vowels ([amplío], etc.). Both classes of verbs are quite large[3] and to my knowledge, no alternative solutions have been proposed to Harris' proposal that verbs of the cambiar type be represented with a stem-final /j/ at the systematic phonemic level.

(2) Words such as áureo, náufrago, láudano, ventrílocuo, which show stress on the fourth from the last orthographic vowel. If the u's in these words are represented as vowels, stress must be placed on the fourth vowel from the end, a pattern which does not exist in Spanish.[4]

In discussing these words, Harris formulates (but ultimately rejects) a phonological rule of glide formation, which might be ordered prior to stress assignment and thereby solve this problem.

However, Harris rejects this solution for the following reasons:

Pairs such as país-paisano, baul-baulero show that Spanish must have a glide formation rule which depends upon stress placement and therefore follows stress assignment. It would be unlikely for a language to have 'two nearly identical rules that cannot be collapsed' (Harris 1969:31), and, more importantly, words like país and baul would be incorrectly reduced to *[pájs] and *[báwl] if there were a glide formation rule ordered before stress assignment.

Harris therefore concludes that only the second rule, the one which follows the stress rule, exists, and that words like láudano, etc. are represented with glides at the systematic phonemic level. Harris' reasoning is, in my opinion, correct insofar as it applies to what Chomsky and Halle (1968:380-389) call 'systematic phonemic matrices'; however, I should like to consider reformulating the rule rejected by Harris as a marking convention and making the claim that, although glides appear in systematic phonemic matrices, no segment need be specifically marked as a glide in the lexicon.[5]

The suggestion has been made at least once that it is possible to combine universal marking conventions and language particular morpheme structure constraints into a single set of rules which relate lexical matrices to phonemic matrices. Furthermore, there seems to be no theoretical obstacle to formulating such a set of rules without making a final determination as to which rules are universal and which are language particular. I will therefore not address myself to the question of whether the rule I am about to formulate expresses a fact about Spanish or a fact about language.

As a substitute for Chomsky and Halle's second and third marking conventions, I propose the two given in (6). Convention 1 makes the claim that the unmarked value of the feature [consonantal] is plus at the beginning of a word and the opposite of the value of the preceding segment otherwise. Convention 2(a) states that the unmarked value of the feature [syllabic] is minus if the segment in question is a high vowel[6] and if it is either preceded or followed by another vowel, and Convention 2(b) states that otherwise the unmarked value of [syllabic] is the opposite of any given segment's value for the feature [consonantal].

(6)

1. $[u \text{ CNS}] \longrightarrow$
$\begin{cases} [+\text{CNS}] \ / \ \# \underline{\hspace{1cm}} & \text{(a)} \\ [\alpha\text{CNS}] \ / \ [-\alpha\text{CNS}] \underline{\hspace{1cm}} & \text{(b)} \end{cases}$

2.

$$[u\ SYL] \rightarrow \left\{ \begin{array}{ll} [-SYL] \ // \ \begin{bmatrix} \underline{} \\ u\ HIG \\ u\ LOW \\ -\ CNS \end{bmatrix} [-\ CNS] & (a) \\[2em] [\alpha\ SYL \ / \ \begin{bmatrix} \\ -\alpha CNS \end{bmatrix} & (b) \end{array} \right.$$

Given these two conventions, it is not necessary to mark the phonetic glides of áureo, láudano, etc. in any manner; however, the high vowels of país, baúl, and other such words will be specified as [m SYL] in the lexicon, and therefore 2(a) will not apply to them. [7]

A strong argument in favor of this approach is that it allows us to mark as less natural items such as país and baúl, which have two contiguous vowels, one of which is high, while leaving V G and G V sequences unmarked. It seems to me that marking lexical items in this way correctly reflects the structure of Spanish words. [8]

The foregoing accounts for one of the types of data mentioned by Harris; however, in order to demonstrate how this marking convention solves the cambiar versus ampliar problem, it will be necessary for me to discuss briefly one difference between my own phonological orientation and what might be called the 'standard generative framework'. Marking conventions are intended (at least partly) to replace morpheme structure rules, and therefore we might assume that they apply to individual morphemes. If this is the case, how can 2(a) apply correctly to the stem /kambi/ converting the /i/ to a glide? Since the /i/ is not contiguous to a vowel in that morpheme, the structural description of 2(a) is not met.

However, for reasons which have nothing to do with glide formation rules, I assume that the application of marking conventions takes place after the spelling out of grammatical morphemes such as theme vowel and other verbal affixes, and after the placement of word boundaries. (That is, marking conventions apply to words, rather than to morphemes.) The motivation for this modification of the standard theory stems from the realization that most of the meaningful constraints on sequences of phonemes in Spanish are constraints upon words: words cannot begin with /r/, nor with two obstruents, words cannot end with two consonants. There are a number of other noncontroversial constraints upon sequences of phonemes in Spanish, and in most cases the meaningful unit is the word. Furthermore, although I have cited several cases in which the meaningful unit must be the word, I know of no case where it must be the morpheme.

Because of this theoretical modification, Convention 2 applies, in my system, after the formation of the words cambiar, cambio, etc. and therefore it applies correctly to them.

As suggested earlier, Convention 2(a) is only one of two glide formation rules which I am proposing for Spanish. Thus I am asserting that the analysis which Harris originally formulated, but rejected, is correct. In order to motivate the inclusion of two glide formation statements which are so similar, it is necessary to show that there are important differences between them. I turn now to a discussion of those differences.

The marking convention formulated applies obligatorily to any vowel sequence which involves a high vowel, unless the high vowel has specifically been excluded by being marked [m SYL]. In every case the rule either applies or it does not apply. There is no choice based upon speed, style, or degree of monitoring. Thus pronunciations such as *[bi-en] and *[bu-en] do not exist.[9]

In contrast to the cases handled by 2(a), when a sequence of vowels involves two nonhigh vowels or is formed as a result of two words coming together, it is necessary to speak of variant pronunciations and to account for them. In (7), I cite a number of examples, giving two pronunciations of each. In this listing, mid vowels which reduce to glides are represented as the corresponding high glides; however, in most dialects a third intermediate pronunciation exists involving a mid glide. Altogether, one might cite four pronunciations of poeta: with a full normal (albeit unstressed) o, with a laxed (or shortened) o, with a mid glide, and with a high glide. This range of possibilities further strengthens the argument that the rule in question is a variable rule.

(7) te - a - tro   tja - tro
     po - e - ta   pwe - ta
     to - a - lla   twa - lla
     mi - a - mor   mja - mor
     tu - e - dad   twe - dad
     te - a do - ro   tja - do - ro

Since it is relatively easy to identify linguistic and sociological factors which are likely determinants of whether or not glide formation occurs in these cases, these instances of glides must be accounted for by a variable rule which is sensitive to the socio-economic and geographical background of the speaker, to the speed of speech, to the position of stress, to the presence of boundaries (and possibly to other factors as well), and which is capable of being applied to strings of words. For the reasons discussed, the other glide formation rule cannot apply to strings of words and must be obligatory. Therefore the two rules cannot be combined and the necessity for two rules is proven.

In conclusion, I should like to offer some speculations on the relationship between variable rules and absolute rules (i.e. rules such as velar softening and palatalization which are not optional). No degree of slowing down, monitoring, or formalization will ever tempt a native speaker of Spanish to say *[lakte] for leche or *[boke] for voz. [10] Yet rules such as these two, and also the absolute glide formation convention, must surely have started out as variable rules. (Recall that one of the early steps in the development of Romance Languages was a shift from patterns like ra-di-o (three syllables) to ra-djo (two syllables with yod).)[11]

From the standpoint of language change, I would like to suggest that rules generally start out as variable rules; however, it is possible for a rule to become absolute. Furthermore, once a rule has become absolute, it is possible for it to be reintroduced as a variable rule, possibly with a somewhat modified environment. Thus I am suggesting that the glide formation rule which I have formulated as a variable rule should be viewed as a reintroduction or, if you wish, a recycled version of the historically earlier rule which yielded the marking convention. [12] Following the well established terminology pattern of 'cyclic', 'pre-cyclic', and 'post-cyclic' rules, one might also speak (diachronically) of 're-cyclic' rules.

NOTES

1. See, in particular, Bowen and Stockwell (1955, 1956) and Saporta (1956). Also, for a good discussion of this controversy, see Alarcos (1965:153ff.).

2. It might be argued that this is precisely the business of phonetics--to describe phonetic differences which are caused by differing environments. However, it seems to me that there is a distinction between an allophonic difference in a particular language (e.g. [b]-[β] alternations in Spanish) and the difference between semi-vowels and semiconsonants which is the 'universal' result of the contact with the other sounds. That is, one can imagine a language without the allophonic conditioning suffered by Spanish /b/, /d/, and /g/, or even with the reverse effects, but it is inconceivable that a language might have sequences such as C SV V or V SC C. Furthermore, there are other types of 'automatic conditioning' phenomena which are not traditionally accounted for by establishing multiple allophones. For example, it can be shown instrumentally that the beginning contour of a vowel (say [a]) is quite different when preceded by, for example [p], from the beginning of that same vowel when preceded by [k].

3. See Harris (1969) for a partial listing of both classes.

4. For an explanation of apparent contradictions to this assertion (e.g. dándonoslo), see Harris (1969:119).

5. Chomsky and Halle make a distinction between 'lexical matrices' and 'phonemic matrices'. The former are the entries which appear in the lexicon and the latter are the result of applying the morpheme structure rules (or marking conventions) to the former. See Chomsky and Halle (1968:380-389). It might be argued that my proposed modification of Harris' analysis is merely 'hair-splitting' since, after all, I agree with his version of the systematic phonemic matrices. However, I feel that if we can define a level of representation which is psychologically meaningful, it must surely be the 'lexical' level. That is, the crucial question is whether native speakers of Spanish control words such as láudano by learning, in each case, that they contain glides. My position is that they do not.

6. For reasons which are beyond the scope of this paper, the configuration [u HIGH, u LOW] refers unambiguously, in my system, to the two high vowels /i/ and /u/. For a discussion of why /a/ cannot also be [u HIGH, u LOW], see Cressey (1970).

7. Neither, incidentally, will it apply to paisano or baulero, since these are comprised of the roots país and baul plus suffixes. This means that these words will have to be correctly glided by the second rule which I propose to discuss below. Since paisano and baulero do not have variable pronunciations (any more than does radio), I consider this fact to be a weakness of my proposals.

8. Furthermore, it is quite conceivable that the convention in question is universal. Chomsky and Halle assume tentatively that this is the case. That is, the effect of Convention 3 (p. 404) is to insure that V G sequences will be less highly marked than V V sequences. This is also pointed out in Harris (1969).

9. It might be claimed that in some cases it is possible to divide diphthongs of this sort and say (complainingly) things like te dije que apagaras la ra-di-o . However, this pronunciation is so unnatural that I take it to be a distortion rather than an overly formal speech style. In any event, there is a clear difference between [ra-di-o] (three syllables) and [te-a-tro] (three syllables) in terms of acceptability.

10. The underlying forms are from Harris (1969).

11. It has been pointed out to me by Harris (personal communication) that, in the light of the Latin Stress Rule, the phonetic glides of láudano, áureo, etc. must already have been glides in Latin, and therefore were not introduced by a variable rule.

12. Similarly the rule which optionally deletes the -d- from first conjugation past participles (hablao, tomao, etc.) might be thought of as a recycling of the historical rule which deleted intervocalic lax

stops. For other instances of rule recycling, see Longmire (forth-coming).

REFERENCES

Alarcos Llorach, Emilio. 1968. Fonología Española. Madrid, Gredos.
Bowen, J. Donald and Robert P. Stockwell. 1955. The phonemic interpretation of semivowels in Spanish. Lg. 31. 236-240.
Bowen, J. Donald and Robert P. Stockwell. 1956. A further note on Spanish semivowels. Lg. 32. 290-292.
Chomsky, Noam and Morris Halle. 1968. The sound pattern of English. New York, Harper and Row.
Cressey, William W. 1970. A note on specious simplifications and the theory of markedness. Papers in Linguistics 2. 227-237.
Harris, James W. 1969. Spanish phonology. Cambridge, Massachusetts, MIT Press.
Harris, James W. 1970. Sequences of vowels in Spanish. Linguistic Inquiry 1. 129-134.
Longmire, Jean. Forthcoming. The relationship of variables in Venezuelan Spanish to differences in style and Venezuelan social class structure.
Navarro Tomás, Tomás. Manual de pronunciación española. Madrid, Consejo Superior de Investigaciones Científicas.
Saporta, Sol. 1956. A note on Spanish semivowels. Lg. 32. 287-290.

ON SUBJECT-RAISING IN SPANISH

MAGDALENA GARCÍA-PINTO
MARTA LUJÁN

The University of Texas at Austin

We find in Spanish many sentences like the following:

(1) Los extranjeros parecen sentir nostalgia de su tierra
'Foreigners seem to feel nostalgia for their land'.
(2) Las mujeres parecen angustiarse con facilidad 'Women
seem to become anguished easily'.
(3) Juan parece disfrutar de sus compañeros de clase
'John seems to enjoy his classmates'.

along with sentences like:

(4) Parece que los extranjeros sienten nostalgia de su tierra
'It seems that foreigners feel nostalgia for their land'.
(5) Parece que las mujeres se anguistian con facilidad 'It
seems that women become anguished easily'.
(6) Parece que Juan disfruta de sus compañeros de clase
'It seems that John enjoys his classmates'.

But while we have:

(7) Parece que los estudiantes hacen el trabajo 'It seems
that the students do the work'.
(8) Parece que esta señora compra el pan allí 'It seems that
this lady buys bread there'.
(9) Parece que María sale ahora 'It seems that Maria goes
out now'.

44

we find the following unacceptable:

(10) *María parece salir ahora 'Maria seems to go out now'.
(11) *Los estudiantes parecen hacer el trabajo 'The students
      seem to do the work'.
(12) *Esta señora parece comprar el pan allí 'This lady
      seems to buy bread there'.

Why are these sentences ungrammatical? The aim of this paper is to
provide a grammatical explanation of the facts pertaining to these
parecer constructions. To this end, we propose an analysis in which
the first two sets of sentences given are transformationally related
by the rule of Subject-Raising. This rule is not only 'triggered' by
the verb parecer, as claimed by Postal (1974), but it must also take
into account some features of the verb in the complement sentence.
We propose that one such feature is [State]. Insofar as our interpretation of the data is adequate, this would indicate that, at least for
Spanish, Postal's assertion that the operation of Raising is largely
controlled by the matrix verb is clearly not sufficient.
   First of all we must establish that sentences like the one in (1)-(3)
are derived structures. To show this we need to show that the noun
phrases with which the main verb agrees are derived subjects, that
is, they are not subjects of the verb parecer in underlying structure.
There is one important syntactic fact that bears on this question.
This concerns the so-called Reflexive-Passive sentences. These
sentences are formed by inserting clitic se and making the verb agree
in number with the direct object. The following sentences illustrate
this construction:

(13) Se pueden decir muchas cosas de Nixon 'Many things can
      be said of Nixon'.
(14) Se planea levantar un edificio encima de Batts Hall
      'It is planned to build a building on top of Batts Hall'.
(15) Se cuentan historias fantásticas de su pasado 'Fantastic
      stories are told of his past'.

Notice that we may also have Reflexive-Passive constructions with
intransitive verbs, and even with the two copulas:

(16) Se duerme bien en el avión 'One sleeps well on the plane'.
(17) Se es bueno y generoso con los amigos 'One is good and
      generous with (his) friends'.
(18) Se está muy cómodamente aquí 'One is comfortable here'.

With the exception of reflexive verbs, practically every sentence that may be used with a human subject can enter into this type of construction. However, no Reflexive-Passives can be formed with verbs that prohibit human subjects:

(19) *Se llueve mucho 'One rains a lot'.
(20) *Se ocurre una desgracia 'One happens a tragedy'.
(21) *Se acontece una catástrofe 'One happens a catastrophe'.

This is in fact the only restriction that this construction obeys, and according to what the facts are with regard to the verb parecer in this construction, we must conclude that this verb does not permit a human subject in deep structure.

(22) *Se parece sentir nostalgia de su tierra 'One seems to feel nostalgia for his land'.
(23) *Se parece angustiarse con facilidad 'One seems to become anguished easily'.
(24) *Se parece disfrutar de los compañeros de clase 'One seems to enjoy (one's) classmates'.
(25) *Se parece bueno 'One seems good'.
(26) *Se parece mal 'One seems badly'.

Clearly then the initial NP's in (1)-(3) are derived subjects. These NP's are deep structure subjects of the verbs in the complements of the verb parecer. We claim that (1)-(3) derive by the rule of Subject-Raising from the same structures as underlie sentences (4)-(6). Basically, this structure is of the following form:

(27)

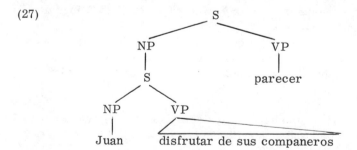

The rule of Subject-Raising takes the embedded subject and raises it to be the matrix subject, at the same time extraposing the remainder of the embedded sentence to be a daughter of the matrix verb phrase.

Postal (1974) has claimed that the operation of Raising is mainly controlled by the superordinate verb, in this case parecer. Hence, from his point of view, the scope of the rule is largely defined by the

superordinate verbal elements which permit the operation of Raising
(Postal 1974:267). But the analysis of the deep structure of the
parecer constructions together with the assumption of the existence
of a grammatical operation of Subject-Raising is clearly not sufficient
to account for all the facts, if we consider a large number of 'raised'
constructions with this verb which are altogether ungrammatical:

(10) *María parece salir ahora.

corresponding to:

(9)   Parece que María sale ahora.
(11) *Los estudiantes parecen hacer el trabajo.

corresponding to:

(7)   Parece que los estudiantes hacen el trabajo.
(12) *Esta señora parece comprar el pan allí.

corresponding to:

(8)   Parece que esta señora compra el pan allí.

If we compare the verbs in the complement sentences of the grammatical 'raised' versions (1)-(3) (divertirse, sentir, angustiarse,
disfrutar) with the verbs in the ungrammatical ones (salir, hacer,
comprar), we may notice that these verbs are semantically and syntactically different. What distinguishes them is their specification
with respect to the feature [State]. The verbs in the complement
sentences of the grammatical 'raised' constructions (1)-(3) are
'stative' verbs while those in the ungrammatical sentences (10)-(12)
are 'nonstative'. Ross (1969) has observed a similar phenomenon in
English: sentences with the verb seem require a 'stative' subordi-
nate verb when used with a for-to complement. He points out that
although

(28) Dr. Mensch seems to know the answer.

is grammatical, it is not possible to say

(29) *Dr. Mensch seems to learn the answer.

The 'stative' verbs which appear in raised constructions with
parecer share some interesting syntactic properties which alone
provide independent motivation for postulating this feature to

subcategorize them. For instance, stative verbs cannot appear in the complement of verbs like <u>persuadir</u> 'persuade', <u>recordar</u> 'remind', <u>sugerir</u> 'suggest', etc.

(30) *Le ⎰persuadí a⎱ que se angustiara.
　　　　⎰recordé ⎱
　　　'I ⎰persuaded⎱ him to become anguished'.
　　　　⎰reminded ⎱

(31) *Le ⎰persuadí a⎱ que disfrutara de sus compañeros.
　　　　⎰recordé ⎱
　　　'I ⎰persuaded⎱ him to enjoy his classmates'.
　　　　⎰reminded ⎱

Nonstative verbs, on the other hand, can be constructed with these matrix verbs:

(32) Le ⎰persuadí a⎱ que viniera pronto.
　　　　⎰recordé ⎱
　　　'I ⎰persuaded⎱ him to come soon'.
　　　　⎰reminded ⎱

(33) Le ⎰persuadí a⎱ que comprara el pan allí.
　　　　⎰recordé ⎱
　　　'I ⎰persuaded⎱ him to buy bread there'.
　　　　⎰reminded ⎱

Second, 'stative' verbs do not permit certain Manner Adverbs:

con entusiasmo	or	entusiastamente
con cortesía	or	cortésmente
con cuidado	or	cuidadosamente
con interés	or	interesadamente
con apatía	or	apáticamente

(34) *Ellos se angustian apáticamente.
　　　'They become anguished apathetically'.
(35) *Ellos sienten nostalgia fríamente.
　　　'They feel nostalgia coldly'.
(36) *Ellos disfrutan cortésmente.
　　　'They enjoy courteously'.

Nonstative verbs, however, can be constructed with such adverbs:

(37) Los rusos recibieron a Nixon cortésmente.
      'The Russians received Nixon courteously'.
(38) Los árabes planearon el tratado cuidadosamente.
      'The Arabs planned the treaty carefully'.
(39) Los argentinos aclamaban a Perón entusiastamente.
      'The Argentinians acclaimed Perón enthusiastically'.

Third, the verbal phrases with stative verbs cannot be pronomi-
nalized by using the verb phrase hacer-lo:

(40) *Manuel se angustió y su hermano también lo hizo.
      'Manuel became anguished and so did his brother'.
(41) *Salomé pareció divertirse y su amante también
      pareció hacerlo.
      'Salome seemed to enjoy herself and so did her lover'.
(42) *Ella pareció entristecerse y también su amigo
      pareció hacerlo.
      'She seemed to become sad and so did her friend'.

However, nonstative verbs do permit this type of pronominalization:

(43) Yo entregué el trabajo ayer y Carmen también lo hizo
      'I handed in the work yesterday and so did Carmen'.
(44) Lily se levantó temprano y su hijo también lo hizo
      'Lilly got up early and so did her son'.
(45) Adela pensaba limpiar la casa y su compañera también
      pensaba hacerlo 'Adela planned to clean up her house
      and so did her roommate'.
(46) Cándido trataba de estudiar y yo también trataba de
      hacerlo 'Candido tried to study and so did I'.

We have shown that verbs must be specified with respect to the
feature State. Given our analysis of the deep structure of sentences
with parecer and the transformational derivation we postulate for the
raised versions, we propose to account for the grammaticality of the
sentences under consideration by claiming that the feature [State] in
the complement verb plays an important role in defining the operation
of Subject-Raising in these sentences. Our proposal is that in order
for this operation to take place it is necessary for the structural
description of this rule to make reference to the specification [+State]
in the main verb of the complement. Thus, although it might be true
that the operation of Raising is mainly controlled by the matrix verb,
it is apparently clear that this is not sufficient for raised sentences
with parecer in Spanish, and according to Ross's observation, for
raised sentences with seem in English.

There are some sentences that appear to contradict our claim. Thus, although the following sentences are ungrammatical:

(10) *María parece salir ahora.
(11) *Los estudiantes parecen hacer el trabajo.
(12) *Esta señora parece comprar el pan allí.

the same sentences with the nonstative verbs salir, comprar, and hacer in the past are grammatical:

(47) María parece haber salido hace una hora.
     'Maria seems to have gone out an hour ago'.
(48) Esta señora parece haber comprado el pan allí.
     'This lady seems to have bought bread there'.
(49) Los estudiantes parecen haber hecho el trabajo.
     'The students seem to have done their work'.

Such sentences would be related to the following sentences, respectively:

(50) Parece que María salió/ha salido hace una hora.
     'It seems that Maria went/has gone out an hour ago'.
(51) Parece que esta señora compró/ha comprado el pan allí.
     'It seems that this lady bought/has bought bread there'.
(52) Parece que los estudiantes hicieron/han hecho su trabajo.
     'It seems that the students did/have done their work'.

These facts do not necessarily force us to abandon our claim. Rather they suggest that the analysis of auxiliaries as main verbs, expounded by Ross (1969), is the correct one. In this light, the main verbs in the complements of these sentences are not salir, comprar and hacer, but the auxiliary of Perfect aspect and Past tense, haber. Since auxiliaries can be shown to be 'stative', their presence in raised constructions with parecer is not only compatible with the set of facts pointed out initially but also predicted by our hypothesis.

REFERENCES

Postal, Paul M. 1974. On raising. Cambridge, MIT Press.
Ross, J. R. 1969. Auxiliaries as main verbs. In: Studies in philosophical linguistics. Edited by W. Todd, series 1.
Ruwet, Nicolas. (to appear). Subject-raising and extraposition. In: Current studies in Romance linguistics. Washington, D.C., Georgetown University Press.

PHONETIC NEUTRALIZATION IN SPANISH AND UNIVERSAL PHONETIC THEORY

JORGE M. GUITART

State University of New York, Buffalo

I would like to comment on the relevance that certain phonetic phenomena in some Caribbean dialects of Spanish may have for a universal phonetic theory.

I would like to explain what I mean by phonetic neutralization. By neutralization in general I mean the exclusion of one or more classes of sounds from a given environment. But a distinction should be made between 'phonological' neutralization and 'phonetic' neutralization. Phonological neutralization is the absence of contrast between systematic phonemes in a given environment. For instance, in English, the contrast between /s/ and any other nonsyllabic segment is neutralized in word-initial position before voiceless obstruents since only /s/ can occur there. Morpheme-structure rules and morpheme-structure constraints are actually phonological neutralization statements. In markedness theory it is argued that most phonological neutralization phenomena are universal and have to do with the limitations of the human speech apparatus (cf. Postal 1968, Chapter 8). I am not concerned here with phonological neutralization and will say no more about it.

Phonetic neutralization, on the other hand, refers to the exclusion of a surface-phonetic segment from a given environment but without any loss of systematic phonemic contrast. All complementary distribution phenomena are instances of phonetic neutralization. More interesting perhaps within phonetic neutralization is the case where the sound that occurs in the surface to the exclusion of others represents two or more systematic phonemes in the same environment and in addition the representative sound is not similar to any of the underlying forms. Still there is no loss of contrast at the systematic phonemic level. I will give an example from Cuban Spanish. In one Havana dialect spoken by uneducated whites, and which I will refer to arbitrarily as Proletarian Habanero, both /s/ and /f/ are 'aspirated' (i. e. realized as a pharyngeal continuant) in preconsonantal position in rapid speech. In addition /r/ is also aspirated before other sonorants, at least word-internally. Examples:

e[h]to for esto 'this'
di[h]teria for difteria 'diphtheria'
ca[h]ne for carne 'meat'
Ca[h]lo for Carlos 'Charles'

The speakers of this dialect know that El a[h]ma de Fidel es automática 'Fidel's gun is automatic' refers to the type of weapon owned by Castro, whereas el a[h]ma del Che se le agravó en Bolivia 'Che's asthma got worse in Bolivia' is a comment on the late Ernesto Guevara's respiratory ailment.

Presumably an utterance such as el a[h]ma es peligrosa 'the weapon is dangerous' or 'asthma is dangerous' could be ambiguous to speakers of this dialect if heard in isolation. But in real life this type of thing does not usually occur. A number of factors such as context, expectation, and redundancy aid the hearer in his 'recovering' the underlying forms from such ambiguous phonic material.

It seems correct to assume that, because so many extraphonetic cues are available to the hearer, the speaker can get away with almost anything in that environment, and in fact he does. Of the relevant features of /s/, /f/, and /r/, only [+continuant] is present, which is perhaps a rather minimal perceptual cue.

Consider now what is involved when it comes to production. As Jakobson, Fant, and Halle (1952) have pointed out, in the production of both [s] and [f], the air must overcome two obstacles: in the case of [s] the constriction of the tongue and the lower teeth; in the case of [f] the upper teeth and the lower lip. That [s] and [f] are such noisy sounds is a consequence of the great degree of energy involved in their production. The production of [h], on the other hand, is obviously a less complicated affair, since no supraglottal obstacle is involved. It is also perhaps less complex physiologically than [r] which calls for rapid tongue activity. In short, it is easier to aspirate all those sounds than not to aspirate them.

In terms of perceptual clarity the speaker is giving up a great deal, for [s] is perhaps the most salient of nonsyllabic sounds, and [r] and [f] are surely clearer signals than [h] (cf. Liberman et al., 1967; Strevens 1960).

There is evidence from perceptual and relative frequency studies that suggests that human speech is most of the time a compromise between speaker and hearer, between perceptual clarity and least effort, favoring heavily one or the other only on infrequent occasions (cf. Saporta 1955; Singh 1968). It seems as if the preconsonantal position in this Cuban dialect is an environment favoring the speaker rather heavily.

Aspiration in Spanish is not the only mechanism available to the speaker who does not need to realize /s/ as an anterior coronal strident in preconsonantal position. There is also deletion, as in [éto] for esto 'this', [mímo] for mismo 'same', heard in Black Cuban. This is of course a very radical solution toward physiological ease. Not so radical is the curious assimilatory process occurring in at least one Puerto Rican dialect spoken in Yabucoa, near Caguas. In this dialect, systematic /s/ is realized in preconsonantal position as an unreleased consonant that copies whatever consonant follows. That is to say, gemination results. Examples:

ca[p'p]a for caspa 'dandruff'
e[t't]o for esto 'this'
de[d'd]e for desde 'from'
lo[b'b]ote for los botes 'the boats'
lo[g'g]ato for los gatos 'the cats'

One interesting thing is that if the second segment is /b, d, g/, the realization is the stop, not the continuant, allophone, which seems logical, physiologically speaking.

We know that /f/ is rather rare in preconsonantal position in Spanish and I haven't heard my Puerto Rican informants say anything with a syllable-final [f], but I would be willing to bet that difteria 'diphtheria' would be rendered di[t't]eria in this dialect.

This type of massive assimilation is put to other uses in certain other Caribbean dialects. For instance, in Proletarian Habanero, the dialect I referred to earlier, gemination occurs in the realization of nonstrident obstruents in syllable-final position in rapid speech. Examples:

do[t't]or for doctor 'doctor'
a[t't]o for both acto 'act' and apto 'fit'
a[d'd]omen for abdomen 'abdomen'

This phenomenon is probably not exclusive of Cuban Spanish, as it is reported by Henriquez Ureña (1940:144) to occur--although infrequently--in Dominican Spanish.

Yet another use for extensive feature assimilation in preconsonantal position occurs in another Havana dialect, my own, which in Guitart (1973) I referred to arbitrarily as the Educated Spanish of Havana, or ESH. In rapid speech in ESH, systematic /l/ and /r/ are realized in closed syllable-final position as the same sound, the nature of which depends totally on the consonant that follows. The coronality or noncoronality of the second consonant seems to play a heavy role here. If the systematic liquid occurs before voiced noncoronal segments, gemination occurs, with the first consonant being unreleased. In addition, if the second consonant is /b, d, g, y/ the stop allophone occurs. Examples:

a[mm]a for both <u>alma</u> 'soul' and <u>arma</u> 'weapon'
e[bʾb]obo for <u>el bobo</u> 'the fool'
se[bʾb]obo for <u>ser bobo</u> 'to be a fool'
e[gʾg]ato for <u>el gato</u> 'the cat'
e[ŷŷ]amó for <u>el llamó</u> 'he called'

If the systematic liquid occurs before voiceless noncoronals, assimilation is equally extensive except that the former liquid remains voiced, thus:

e[bʾp]adre for <u>el padre</u> 'the father'
e[gʾk]aso for <u>el caso</u> 'the case'

If the second consonant is [+coronal], then the former liquid is realized also as a coronal but a nonanterior one. In addition the second consonant becomes [-anterior] too. Before /s/, the former liquid is realized as a flap (which we transcribe arbitrarily as [ɾ̈]), before other coronals as a nonanterior d ([d̈]), which is unreleased. True gemination occurs when the second consonant is /d/. Examples:

e[d̈ʾd̈]omingo for <u>el domingo</u> 'Sunday'
prime[d̈ʾd̈]omingo for <u>primer domingo</u> 'first Sunday'
e[ɾ̈š]ocio for <u>el socio</u> 'the partner'
se[ɾ̈š]ocio for <u>ser socio</u> 'to be a partner'

The fact that the second consonant becomes nonanterior alters its timbre, especially in the case of /s/, with [š] sounding more similar to English [ŝ] than to English [s].

It is interesting that the same process of assimilation is used in three different varieties of Caribbean Spanish for three different purposes: as a representation of systematic /s/ in one dialect, of all nonstrident obstruents in a second dialect, and of both liquids in a third dialect. This suggests perhaps that we are dealing with a somewhat general process. The fact that it occurs in rapid speech but not in slower tempos strikes me as an indication of naturalness. It might be interesting to measure, say by electromyography, the muscular activity involved in my articulating the utterance el fonólogo debería saber fonética 'the phonologist should know phonetics' as I would read it, without liquid assimilation, and then as I would say it in rapid speech: e[ff]onólogo debería sabe[ff]onética. It seems quite obvious that a sequence of two sounds sharing many features, especially those pertaining to tongue movements, should be physiologically less complex than a sequence of dissimilar segments. And there is yet another way in which assimilations of the type described should be considered less complex. If articulated speech is produced by a series of neutral instructions, it seems intuitively correct to assume that it is simpler to have the same set of instructions for different segments than to have different sets of instructions. For the empirical confirmation or disconfirmation of some of these assumptions, we will have to wait until some experimental phonetician or neurologist of the hopefully not very distant future takes an active interest in phonological theory.

REFERENCES

Guitart, J. M. 1975. Markedness and a Cuban dialect of Spanish. Georgetown University Working Paper on Languages and Linguistics. Number 10. Washington, D.C., Georgetown University Press.

Honríquez Ureña, P. 1940. El español do Santo Domingo. Biblioteca de Dialectología Hispanoamericana, V. Buenos Aires, Instituto de Filología.

Jakobson, R., C. Gunnar Fant, and M. Halle. 1952. Preliminaries to speech analysis. Cambridge, MIT Press.

Liberman, A. M., F. S. Cooper, D. P. Shakweiler, and M. Studdert-Kennedy. 1967. Perception of the speech code. Psychological Review 74.431-61.

Postal, P. M. 1968. Aspects of phonological theory. New York, Harper and Row.

Saporta, S. 1955. Frequency of consonant clusters. Language 31.25-30.

Singh, S. 1968. A distinctive feature analysis of responses to a multiple-choice intelligibility test. International Review of Applied Linguistics 6.37-53.

Strevens, P. 1960. Spectra of fricative noise in human speech. Language and Speech 3.32-49.

STRESS ASSIGNMENT RULES IN SPANISH

JAMES W. HARRIS

Massachusetts Institute of Technology

1. Introduction. A study of generative stress assignment rules in Spanish was included in my book <u>Spanish Phonology</u> (1968, hereafter <u>SpPh</u>). This study, however, did not pretend to be either exhaustive or definitive. More than half a decade has passed without comprehensive reexamination of the subject, as far as I know. The purpose of the present paper is to reopen for discussion the topic of stress assignment in Spanish, to review certain partial proposals that have appeared recently, to present new proposals of my own, and in passing, to rectify certain misinterpretations of <u>SpPh</u> that have arisen.

One of the central claims of <u>SpPh</u> concerning stress was that the principles governing stress in verbs are at least partially distinct from those that govern stress in nonverb forms. No evidence has appeared that contradicts this claim. However, the <u>SpPh</u> proposals for both verb and nonverb stress must be revised, and the two sets of principles will be discussed largely independently of one another in Section 3 (nonverbs) and 4 (verbs). For the sake of clarity, I will present at the outset some justification for discussing these separately, even though the arguments given in <u>SpPh</u> remain valid after the rules are revised, as will be seen.

2. Verb stress versus nonverb stress. In <u>SpPh</u> (120) a long but not exhaustive list is given of examples like those in (1):

(1) | <u>Noun, Adjective</u> | <u>Verb</u> |
|---|---|
| contínuo 'continuous' | continúo 'I continue' |
| próspero 'prosperous' | prospéro 'I prosper' |
| vómito 'vomit' | vomíto 'I vomit' |

práctica 'practice, practical'   practíca '(he) practices'
partícipe 'participant'   participíe '(he) participates'
                                              (subjunctive)

All the nouns and adjectives in (1) have antepenultimate stress, while
all the corresponding otherwise homophonous verb forms have penultimate stress. Thus either (a) at the stage of derivation at which stress
is assigned, the segmental composition of the forms of one or both
sets differs in some relevant respect from the segmental composition
of the corresponding surface representations, or (b) different stress
rules are involved. Since no evidence for (a) is known--that is, since
stress is assigned to representations that are identical in all relevant
respects to surface representations--it follows that the stress rules
for verbs are not identical to those for nonverbs.

3. Stress assignment in nonverb forms. Let us now temporarily
disregard verb forms entirely. Furthermore, in our exclusive concern with nonverb forms, let us pretend for the moment that we are
totally ignorant of the existence of the well-known Latin or Romance
Stress Rule. In short, let us begin from scratch to develop an account
of stress assignment for nonverb forms in Spanish.
As a matter of elementary methodological principle, one must
determine which stress patterns native speakers consider to be
grammatical or well formed and which, if any, they consider to be
ungrammatical or ill formed. (A grammar must account for at least
this much, even if it cannot achieve greater refinement.) As a matter
of fact, Spanish draws a fairly clear line between admissible and in
admissible stress patterns: all Spanish words, regardless of origin
and date of entry into the language, receive primary stress on one of
the last three syllables. [1] Letting pa represent an arbitrary open
syllable, it can be said that words are found of the types . . . pápapa,
. . . pápa, and . . . pá, but there are no words, however marginal,
of the type *. . . pápapapa. It follows, then, that the stress rules of
Spanish are limited to at most the three shown in (2), whatever further
constraints may be imposed on these: [2]

(2)
$$V \rightarrow [+\text{stress}] / \begin{cases} \overline{S} - S - S \; \#]_{\alpha} & \text{(a)} \\ \underline{S} - S \; \#]_{\alpha} & \text{(b)} \\ S \; \#]_{\alpha} & \text{(c)} \end{cases}$$

Rule (2a) must be refined immediately, since it is too general.
Words whose penultimate syllable is closed may not have antepenultimate stress. Abstractly, there are no words like *pápampa, whose
syllable division are pa-pam-pa. [3] In general, obstruent-plus-liquid
clusters are syllabified together with the following vowel. Thus

antepenultimate stress may be found in words like múltiple 'multiple' fúnebre 'funereal', etc., whose penultimate syllable is open, though followed by two [+consonantal] segments. Native speakers readily reject made-up items like *tánaspo, *múltinde, etc. as ill formed, while accepting as potential words equally nonexistent forms like tánabro, pétiple. The exclusion of words like *pápampa is thus clearly part of the native speakers' tacit competence, and must therefore be represented in the rules of the grammar. Therefore (2a) is replaced by (3), which permits antepenultimate stress only in words whose penultimate syllable is open:

(3) $V \rightarrow [\text{+stress}] \; / \; \bar{S} - C_0 V - S \;\#]_\alpha$

Rules (3), (2b), and (2c) apply in the order just listed, and they apply disjunctively, according to any and all of the various familiar proposals regarding disjunctive ordering. Thus, all words that fail to undergo (3) are then subject to (2b, c).

No general exclusions exist other than those just discussed. Both antepenultimately and penultimately stressed words not violating (3) are common: abstractly, both the types pápap(L)a and papáp(L)a are plentiful. It is not too difficult to find nearly minimal pairs (of real words) like epístola/pistóla 'epistle'/'pistol', nómada/pomáda 'nomad'/ 'pomade, salve', estrambótica/botíca 'extravagant'/'pharmacy', and even absolutely minimal pairs like sábana/sabána 'sheet'/'savanna, treeless plain'. The morphological structure of both sábana and sabána is simply the root /saban/ plus the 'gender vowel' a which is typical of feminine nouns and adjectives. Thus there can exist no general independent phonological or morphological property on the basis of which the position of stress can be predicted in the set of words in question. Evidently, some special mark must be supplied in the lexical representations of the words in question that determines whether they receive penultimate or antepenultimate stress.

What must be the nature of this mark? As a first guess, one might suggest the most 'concrete' interpretation possible, namely, that the lexical mark in question is the feature [+stress] itself. However, this idea collapses immediately in the face of examples like teléfono 'telephone' (noun), telefónico 'telephone, telephonic' (adjective), telefonísta 'telephone operator', and telegráma, 'telegram', which are typical of a very wide class of cases. Take teléfono; one cannot say that the second e is inherently or lexically stressed, for the simple reason that it occurs unstressed in telefónico, telefonísta, telegráma, etc. Suppose one denies that the telé- of teléfono is the same morpheme as the tele- of telefónico, telefonista, etc. (or, more extremely, denies that the teléfon- of teléfono is the same as the telefón- of telefónico or the telefon- of telefonísta), or claims instead that 'words' rather than morphemes are lexically marked for stress. The first of these claims is patently ludicrous, I would say; and the second is forced to miss the generalization that all words ending in the suffix -ico '-ic' receive stress on the syllable immediately preceding this suffix, the generalization that all words ending in the suffix -ista '-ist' are penultimately stressed, and in fact every other generalization about stress placement in Spanish.

Other straw men are available for decapitation, but I will desist. I know of no workable alternative to the following: every vowel that appears unstressed in the penultimate syllable of the phonetic representation of any form is assigned in the lexicon the abstract diacritic feature [X]. For example, the lexical representation of the morpheme fón in teléfono, telefónico, etc., is /fon/, and that of ic is /ɨk/. The only interpretation attached to the diacritic [X] is that it serves to trigger application of the rule (3) that assigns penultimate stress, which is accordingly revised as shown in (4):

(4) $\quad V \rightarrow [+\text{stress}] / \bar{S} - C_0[X] - S \#]_\alpha$

The application of (4) to teléfono and telefónico is illustrated in (5):

(5) $\quad$ /tel e f ó no/ $\qquad$ /telef ó n i ko/

with X marked over the ó vowels; $-C_0X- S\#$ and resulting é, ó.

The effect of the diacritic [X] is thus not the absolute prohibition of stress assignment to a vowel so marked but effects such a prohibition only when a vowel marked [X] happens to occur in a penultimate syllable.[4] It should be obvious that the presence of [X] in no way affects the assignment of penultimate stress by rule (2b) in such a word as telefonísta, as is illustrated in (6):

(6) $\quad$ /telef ó nis ta/ (with X over ó)

$\qquad -C_0X- S \#$ $\qquad$ (4) not applicable

$\qquad \quad - S \#$ $\qquad$ (2b)

resulting í.

There is a claim implicit in the proposal just outlined which is by no means accidental and which therefore should be mentioned explicitly. Words with an open penultimate syllable require no special mark in order for stress to be assigned to that syllable. (The same is true of course of words with a closed penultimate syllable.) On the other hand, words with an open penultimate syllable do require a special mark in order for stress to be assigned to the antepenultimate syllable. The obvious, and intended, interpretation of this situation is that penultimate stress is the expected, literally 'unmarked', case whereas antepenultimate stress is the special, literally 'marked', case. There is some evidence that this interpretation is correct, and an accurate reflection of native speaker competence:

(a) Borrowings whose original pronunciation is not maintained by normative influences are given penultimate stress (barring countervailing factors such as accidental similarity to a native word); e.g. 'Colgate', 'Palmolive'--common trade names in some countries--and 'detective' are pronounced [koɣáte], [palmolíβe], [detektíβe].

(b) In informal tests, native speakers stress phonologically admissible nonsense words on the penultimate syllable (again barring extraneous influences).

(c) There are numerous examples of spontaneous historical changes from antepenultimate to penultimate stress in paradigmatically isolated words, e.g. árabe > arábe, héroe > heróe, Gerónimo > Geronímo, etc. but few or no changes in the opposite direction that cannot be attributed to some specific extraneous factor. [5] A straightforward interpretation of this asymmetry is the loss of the special mark [X].

For whatever the observation is worth, it might also be noted that the official orthography--one of the best in the world--leaves penultimate stress unmarked but marks stress in all other positions.

Returning to the main thread of the exposition, polysyllabic words with stress on the final syllable remain to be discussed. One may distinguish two classes of cases, (a) words like papél/papéles 'paper(s)' and (b) words like papá/papás 'daddy(-ies)'.

In SpPh I proposed that words like papél/papéles be derived as illustrated in (7):

(7)
Singular	Plural	
/papel+e/	/papel+e+s/	
é	é	Stress (2b)
∅		Apocope
papél	papéles	

As illustrated, stress is assigned to the penultimate syllable of the representation to which the stress rule applies. Thus words like papél are not exceptions to the 'normal' rule of penultimate stress placement (2b).

The claim to nonexceptional status for papél-type words is justified to the extent that no part of the description of stress placement illustrated in (7) is ad hoc. What is crucial, of course, is the final /+e/ of singular forms and the Apocope rule that deletes this segment in singular forms. Both would still be motivated even if stress placement in Spanish were radically different from what it is--say, if stress regularly fell on the first syllable of every word. The final +e of underlying representations like /papel+e/ is inserted by morphological or word-formation rules in accordance with which all fully regular nouns and adjectives end in

(a) -o: masculine, e.g. sobrino 'nephew', rico 'rich'
(b) -a: feminine, e.g. sobrina 'niece', rica
(c) -e: either gender, e.g. padre, madre, inteligente

Now consider the asymmetry in the following array of forms, specifically the 'blank' in (8c iii):

(8)

		Singular	Plural
	(a)	sobrin+o	sobrin+o+s 'nephew(s)'
	(b)	sobrin+a	sobrin+a+s 'niece(s)'
	(c i)	padr+e	padr+e+s 'father(s)'
	(c ii)	petat+e	petat+e+s 'mat(s)'
	(c iii)	papel__	papel+e׀s 'paper(s)'

The 'gender vowels' -o, -a, -e appear in all plural forms, and the plural morpheme is invariably -s. In the singular forms, the gender vowel appears as expected in (8a, b). Furthermore, in singulars whose 'gender vowel' is -e, this segment appears after any cluster of nonsyllabic segments (8c i) and after any voiceless consonant (8c ii) but is not present after a single voiced dental [+consonantal] segment (8c iii). This final case is clearly the special one, and it thus provides clear motivation for a rule of Apocope that deletes word-final -e after a single voiced dental consonant. [6]

The residual class of final-stressed words like papá/papás consists of a relatively small number of partially assimilated loan words, along with a few fully native words; e.g. ballet [balét], hindú, carnét [karnét] 'ID card', debut [deβút], mamá, papá. For most speakers the plurals of these words are ballets [baléts], hindús, carnets [karnéts], debuts [deβúts], mamás, papás. Thus, unlike the papél/papéles type, these residual words cannot have stems ending in -e in underlying representations since this -e would appear phonetically in plurals like *balletes *[balétes], *hindúes, mamáes, etc.

In SpPh, papá-type words were considered to be simply exceptions to the penultimate stress rule (2b), thus undergoing the final rule (2c)-- and that was the end of the matter. I have considered a number of alternatives, but since I can argue for none of them with much conviction, I will let the subject rest at this point. [7]

As those familiar with SpPh will have recognized, the account just sketched of stress assignment for nonverb forms does not differ markedly from that of SpPh, although the presentation is superficially quite different. There is a larger context, however, in which I reject one of the generalizations of SpPh. Rule (4) makes use of an arbitrary diacritic [X], just as the analogous rule in SpPh (121, passim) makes use of the arbitrary diacritic [D]. SpPh furthermore made use of the diacritic [D] in determining the diphthongization of mid vowels under stress and in several other processes. [8]

It now seems clear, however, that the interesting generalization that one and the same diacritic feature is relevant both for stress placement and for diphthongization (and other processes) must be abandoned. A small sample of the type of evidence that is crucial is provided by words like:

Venezuéla 'Venezuela'	venezoláno 'Venezuelan'
consuélo 'consolation'	consolár 'to console'
sosiégo 'calm, quiet' (noun)	sosegádo 'calm, quiet' (adjective)
travíeso 'mischievous'	travesúra 'mischief'

The underlying diphthongs ué, ié alternate with o, e, respectively. Other phonetically identical o's and e's do not alternate. Therefore some diacritic feature distinguishes diphthongizing from nondiphthongizing o and e. [9] Call this diacritic [D]. Now a problem arises if one assumes that [D] is the same as the diacritic [X] discussed in connection with (4), (5), and (6): the penultimate vowel of Venezuéla, consuélo, etc. must be marked [D] = [X] to account for the diphthong (from venezóla, consóla, roughly) but must not be marked [D] = [X] for stress to be assigned to the penultimate syllable. There is no motivation at all for claiming that the penultimate syllable is closed in the representation to which stress applies, as is clearly the case in words like pariénte 'relative'--cf. parentéla '(set of) relatives'. We must therefore abandon the assumption that [D] = [X]. I of course pointed out in SpPh that sets of words like traviéso/travesúra, etc. were not consistent with the assumption in question, but, for reasons that are no longer relevant, I held out the hope that some way around such examples would be found. The burden of proof rests on anyone who would claim that [D] = [X], and I know of no way in which the challenge could be met.

It has been stated a number of times that it is claimed in SpPh that stress is assigned to nonverb forms by the so-called Latin Stress Rule. [10] However, the position actually taken in SpPh (see for example, 30-31, 118-120) was that something like the Latin Stress Rule has just enough right with it to be taken as a first hypothesis and just enough wrong with it to preclude uncritical acceptance. Rule (4), like its counterpart in SpPh, bears a striking similarity to the Latin Stress Rule, but in point of technical fact it would be incoherent to say that (4) 'is' the Latin Stress Rule (or more accurately, one of its cases) since (4) makes reference to the arbitrary, nonphonological diacritic feature [X] while the Latin Stress Rule makes reference to the phonological property of long versus short vowels, a property that is of no relevance whatsoever in Spanish.

4. Stress assignment in verb forms. Spanish verb forms, like nonverb forms, can be stressed only on one of the last three syllables. [11] According to SpPh, antepenultimate stress in certain verb forms, e.g. trabajábamos, is assigned by a rule that refers to the syntactic-semantic feature [-perfective]. That is, the rule in question depends on the identification of a morpheme manifesting 'imperfective aspect' in verb forms. Problems with this formulation were pointed out in SpPh (77-78), namely, some of the supposedly imperfective morphemes in question may not be imperfective; and more than one critic has voiced objections to which I plead nolo contendere. [12] I will argue now that the correct formulation is no less dependent on morphological information but refers to the verbal 'theme vowel' rather than to an aspectual morpheme. In a 'historical excursus' appended, I will sketch certain stages in the evolution of the stress patterns of Spanish verb forms and will discuss the bearing of this material on certain theoretical issues of current interest.

Although stress is assigned to representations of verb forms that are in all relevant respects identical to surface phonetic representations, the discussion to follow will be facilitated by a brief sketch of the morphology of verb forms. [13] Overlooking a few irrelevant details (for example, the fact that verb stems often contain prefixes and certain derivational affixes), we may say that verb forms are composed morphologically as shown in (9):

$$(9)\quad [\ [\ [\text{Root}] + \begin{bmatrix}\text{Theme}\\ \text{Vowel}\end{bmatrix}]_{\text{Stem}} \left\{ \begin{array}{l} +[\text{Ending}]\ ]_{\text{Verb}} \\[2ex] +\begin{bmatrix}\text{Tense-}\\ \text{Mood-}\\ \text{Aspect}\end{bmatrix} + \begin{bmatrix}\text{Person-}\\ \text{Number}\end{bmatrix}]_{\text{Verb}} \end{array} \right.$$

Non-finite forms (Infinitive, Past Participle, Gerund)

Finite forms (those marked for person and number)

The internal brackets in (9) are used only to identify morphological constituents and carry no implication of cyclical application of rules.

To partially illustrate (9), consider the root limpi 'clean'. This can occur with a 'gender vowel' to form the adjective limpio/limpia 'clean', whose structure is $[[\text{limpi}]_{rt} + \text{o/a}]_{Adj}$. The same root can also occur with the suffix -ez- plus a 'gender vowel' to form the feminine noun limpieza 'cleanness, cleaning', whose structure is roughly $[[\text{limpi}] + \text{ez} + \text{a}]_N$. Also, limpi can occur with a 'theme vowel', to form a verb stem limpia- 'clean', $[[\text{limpi}]_{rt} + [\text{a}]_{th}]_{stem}$, to which verbal inflections are added. One makes the following assumptions about (9):

(a) Roots are listed in the Lexicon, where the appropriate semantic, syntactic, morphological (e.g. conjugational class affiliation), and phonological information is given.

(b) Theme vowels are supplied by morphological rule: /a/, /e/, /i/ for first, second, and third conjugation roots, respectively.

(c) Tense-Mood-Aspect and Person-Number morphemes consist of bundles of syntactic features assigned by syntactic rules.

(d) The arrangements of morphemes represented schematically in (9) are governed by 'word-formation rules' of the morphological component of the grammar, and morpho-syntactic representations of the sort mentioned in (c) are converted into phonological (phonemic) representations by other rules of the morphological component.

With this much background, it can now be observed that most verb forms are stressed on the penultimate syllable, as illustrated in (10) with the first conjugation (theme vowel a) root trabaj- 'work':[14]

(10a) past participle: trabajádo
(10b) gerund: trabajándo
(10c) present indicative: trabájo,[15] trabájas, trabajámos, trabája, etc.
(10d) present subjunctive: trabáje,[15] trabájes, trabajémos, etc.
(10e) imperfect: trabajába, trabajábas, etc.
(10f) past subjunctive: trabajára/trabajáse, trabajáras/ trabajáses, etc.
(10g) preterit: trabajáste, trabajámos, trabajáron

It is important to note that the vowel of the stressed penultimate syllable in (10) is variously the theme vowel (trabaj+á+do, trabaj+á+ndo), the last vowel of the root (trabáj+o, trabáj+a+s), the present subjunctive morpheme (trabaj+é+mos). In other forms, a wider variety of morphological elements is found in stressed penultimate syllables. For example, in several athematic past participles like cubiérto, the past participle of cubr- 'cover' (infinitive cubrir), the stressed vowel is inorganic, being inserted by an automatic, exceptionless rule, as illustrated in (11):

(11) cubr + to
      cuber to $\emptyset \rightarrow e$ / C _____ rC (cf. cobertúra 'cover, covering')
      cubér to Stress
      cubiérto Diphthongization

In certain suppletive forms, it is difficult, and perhaps totally arbitrary, to assign the stressed vowel to any particular morphological constituent; for example éres, sómos (idiosyncratic present indicative forms whose infinitive is ser 'to be'); estúve, andúve, estuvímos, anduvímos (preterit forms of st+a- 'be', and and+a- 'go, walk'). Evidently then, no morphological condition must or can be placed on the rule for penultimate stress in verb forms. This rule should be formulated simply as in (12):

(12) $V \rightarrow [\text{+stress}] / \bar{S} - S \#]_{\beta}$

The 'β' in (12) is a shorthand notation to refer to all the categories subsumed under 'α' in rule (2), plus verb forms. In other words, one simply extends rule (2b) to include verb forms, making this the 'all purpose' penultimate stress rule. It may also be noted immediately that there are a fair number of (stressed) monosyllabic verb forms (e. g. dá, és, dén, són, vá, dóy, hán, só, sál, dí, ház, etc.), and hence an 'all purpose' counterpart to (2c). In short, the 'all purpose' version of (2c) and rule (12) can be collapsed as in (13):[16]

(13) $V \rightarrow [\text{+stress}] / \bar{S} (- S) \#]_{\beta}$

Turn now to antepenultimately stressed verb forms. This set of forms is morphologically much more homogeneous than penultimately and final-syllable stressed ones, as is shown in (14), again using trabaj - to illustrate:

(14a) imperfect: trabaj+á+ba+mos, trabaj+á+ba+is
(14b) past subjunctive: trabaj+á+ra+mos, trabaj+á+ra+is
       (some dialects): trabaj+á+se+mos, trabaj+á+se+is

(14c) preterit: trabaj+á +steis

The forms ending in -mos are first person plural; those ending in -is are second person plural.[17] The stressed vowel is the theme vowel in all cases. The forms illustrated in (14) are all and only those in which the theme vowel is followed by two inflectional syllables. Thus the rule for antepenultimate stress in verb forms may be stated as in (15):

$$(15) \quad V \rightarrow [+\text{stress}] \ / \ \left.\begin{array}{c} \overline{S} \\ [\text{ThV}] \end{array}\right]_{\text{St}} \left.\begin{array}{c} S - S \# \\ \\ \end{array}\right]_{\text{Verb}}$$

It should be noted that (15) assigns stress correctly to second person plural preterit forms, e.g. [[trabaj + a]$_{St}$ + ste - is] $\rightarrow$ trabajásteis. The SpPh rule, which required an imperfective morpheme in the penultimate syllable, could not handle this case, since preterit forms are perfective.[18]

To recapitulate quickly: The bulk of Spanish verb forms are stressed by the rules (15) and (13). Rule (15), the antepenultimate rule, applies first to a homogeneous set of forms, namely, those in which two inflectional syllables follow the theme vowel. All remaining forms, regardless of their morphological structure, undergo (13), the general penultimate and monosyllable stress rule that applies to all stressable categories of forms. Rule (15), like (4), is disjunctive with respect to (13), this disjunctivity being imposed by any and all of the familiar principles based on parenthesizability, 'elsewhere', proper inclusion, etc.

There are certain forms whose surface representation is opaque with respect to rule (13), that is, stress is not penultimate in the surface representations of these forms. I will consider each case briefly.

First, infinitives, for example trabajár 'to work', which are stressed on the final syllable in surface representations, seem to violate rule (13). Actually they do not, however. Consider (16):

(16) [[trabaj+a]+r]
      [[trabaj+a]+r+e] $([+N, \ +V, \ \ldots])$ General morphological rule
      trabaj a r e   Stress: (12)
      trabajár   Apocope

The justification of every step in this derivation is quite straightforward. Infinitives have traditionally been called 'verbal nouns' since they share a good bit of syntactic behavior with nouns (more so in Spanish than in English, where gerunds have some of the functions that infinitives have in Spanish) although they are of course not syntactically indistinguishable from nouns. For example, Spanish infinitives may function as subjects and predicate nominals (ver es creer 'seeing is believing'), they may be objects of prepositions (sin ver 'without seeing'), they may have articles (el hacerlo 'doing it, the doing of it'), they may have plurals like nouns and adjectives (andares 'goings about', decires 'sayings'), and so on. Notice that the final -e shown in (16) appears phonetically in the plural forms, which is its main justification. Furthermore, this final -e comes without any cost whatsoever, since it is inserted by the same general morphological rule that adds a final -e to all nouns and adjectives (e.g. padre, madre, inteligente) to which is not added the typical 'gender vowel' -o for masculine gender (tío 'uncle') or -a for feminine gender (tía 'aunt'). After stress is assigned, final -e is deleted by an Apocope rule that deletes word-final -e under certain conditions in nouns and adjectives.[19] In sum, the classification of infinitives as verbal nouns, more specifically [+N, +V, ...], which is apparently demanded in any event on syntactic grounds, automatically accounts for the seemingly odd fact that infinitives undergo an Apocope rule restricted to nouns and adjectives, and it also tells us why infinitives have an underlying final -e in the first place, which permits them to be stressed in the normal way by (12), that is, the penultimate case of the general rule (13).

Second, regular preterit first and third person singular forms have stress on the final syllable in phonetic representations, e.g. first conjugation (a-theme) trabajé 'I worked', trabajó '(he) worked'; third conjugation (i-theme) salí 'I went out', salió '(he) went out'. Derivations of these forms are given in (17), as well as derivations of the irregular preterit forms púde and púdo for comparison:[20]

(17)

1st person singular			3rd person singular			
trabaj+a+i	sal+i+i	pod+i	trabaj+a+u	sal+i+u	pod+u	
		pudi			pudu	$[-\text{low}] \rightarrow [+\text{hi}]$ in irreg prets
trabajei			trabajou			$a \rightarrow \begin{Bmatrix} e/\text{—}i \\ o/\text{—}u \end{Bmatrix}$
trabajéi	salíi	púdi	trabajóu	salíu	púdu	Stress (13)
trabajé	salí		trabajó			$\begin{bmatrix} +\text{high} \\ \alpha\text{back} \end{bmatrix} \rightarrow \emptyset \ / \ \begin{bmatrix} -\text{low} \\ \alpha\text{back} \end{bmatrix}$ __
		púde		salió	púdo	Lowering
				salió		Stress Shift
trabajé	salí	púde	trabajó	salió	púdo	

The derivations in (17) are similar to those of preterit forms given in SpPh (79-86) but not identical. The following observations may be made:

(a) Forms of trabaj- and sal-, which are regular, consist of the stem (=root plus theme vowel) followed by a person-number inflection; forms of pod-, which are irregular, do not have a theme vowel but do have the regular person-number endings.

(b) The SpPh rule of Lowering (84, passim), has been revised in Harris (1973). The new formulation makes no reference to any arbitrary diacritic, and it applies to verb forms only, lowering unstressed i̱ to e̱ and u̱ to o̱ in the final syllable.

For the sake of argument, I am willing to grant that all the rules illustrated in (17) except Stress are ad hoc in the sense that they have no motivation outside preterit forms, although I am firmly convinced that this concession is excessively generous. Be that as it may, the derivations in (17) are still attractive and reasonably well motivated, given the regularity of the underlying representations and the wide divergence between these representations and the surface representations. In other words, it is difficult to see how the same data could be accounted for with fewer or better motivated rules. In fact, no explicitly formulated alternative account has yet appeared in the literature, and one must therefore let the matter rest until another proposal is offered whose merits can be determined. [21]
Finally, all future tense forms of all verbs except first and second person plural have stress on the final syllable: trabajaré, trabajarás, trabajará, trabajarán (along with first and second plural trabajarémos, trabajaréis). In SpPh (91-96) phonological, morphological, syntactic, and semantic arguments were given for considering future (and conditional) verb forms to be composites consisting of the infinitive followed by a form of the idiosyncratic auxiliary verb haber. The structure of future forms was taken to be roughly that illustrated in (18):

(18) [[trabajar] [he]]   [[trabajar] [has]]

The brackets in (18) are real ones, which impose cyclical assignment of stress. Thus the final stress of trabajaré, trabajarás, etc. is simply the consequence of the assignment of stress by rule (13) to the monosyllabic rightmost constituent. I can no longer place much confidence in the syntactic and semantic arguments presented in SpPh. If these are discarded, then some of the motivation for the structures illustrated in (18) disappears. More specifically, if sentences containing future verb forms are not derived syntactically from abstract

structures in which a form of haber appears as an independent verb,
then there is no syntactic motivation for the claim that the rightmost
constituents in (18) are literally forms of haber. There are, on the
other hand, morphological and phonological arguments for (18) that
cannot be dismissed lightly. For example, future 'stems'--more
accurately, the leftmost constituents of (18)--have the same surface
forms as infinitives, even in cases of suppletion (e. g. seré, iré, etc.),
and future 'endings' are identical to the idiosyncratic independent
present indicative forms of haber. On purely methodological grounds,
one should take the strongest possible position, namely, that the
SpPh analysis involving (18) is correct, until it is shown to be untenable. However, for the sake of argument, let us assume, contrary to fact, that conclusive syntactic and/or semantic evidence
against this position is available. To what weaker position shall we
retreat? Let us grant that the phonetic identity of future 'endings'
and independent forms of haber is a synchronic coincidence whose
only proper explanation is historical. (Incidentally, the historical
explanation is known to be correct.) Even so, we must replace (18)
with structures of no less complexity than those shown in (19):

(19) [[trabajar] + e]   [[trabajar] + as]

The intended interpretation of (19) is that the inner constituents are in
fact infinitives, and the 'endings' or outer constituents are simply the
phonological realizations of the feature [+future] supplied by the morphological component. The amount of structure shown in (19) is
justified by facts like the following (which I would hesitate to call
'historical accidents'). The future forms of the stem oi- 'hear',
oiré, oirás, oirémos, etc., are phonetically [oiré], [oirás],
[oirémos], etc.; not *[oyré], *[oyrás], *[oyrémos], etc. Since
there is a well-known general rule of 'glide formation' that converts
unstressed high vowels into glides when they are adjacent to another
vowel, one must ask why this rule does not apply to oiré [oiré], etc.
With structures of the type shown in (19), there is no problem: on
the inner cycle stress is assigned to the (then penultimate) i of the
infinitive oir(e); the glide-formation rule is thus blocked since it
applies only to unstressed vowels. Similar, but independent, odd
phonological wrinkles of future tense forms that fall out as automatic
consequences of the structure shown in (19)--or (18)--are mentioned
in SpPh (95-96, 111).

It is important to observe that structures of the type (19), or some
notational equivalent, must be generated by the morphological component in any event, quite independently of future tense verb forms.
In Harris (1974:section 2. 2) there is detailed discussion of a number
of reasonably clear cases, all of which share with future verb forms

the property of containing within a single larger phonological word an 'island' consisting of the surface representation of a smaller word (the infinitive is the contained 'island' in the future verb forms). In short, the analysis of future forms just sketched appears to be well motivated; it accounts simultaneously for a range of disparate facts, including the apparently exceptional final stress of future tense forms. As was the case with the preterit forms discussed above, no explicitly formulated alternative that takes into consideration the same range of data has been proposed, as far as I know.

To summarize this section: All verb forms are stressed by the disjunctive set of rules (15) and (13), which apply in that order.

5. Historical excursus. There are several substandard Latin American dialects in which the placement of stress in verb forms is not quite the same as in standard dialects. For the sake of convenience, I refer to these nonstandard dialects as 'retracting' dialects. [22] Illustrative paradigms from standard and retracting dialects are given in (20), with singular forms in the left column and plural in the right in the usual way:

(20)   Standard   Retracting

(a) Present   trabájo   trabajámos
    indicative   trabájas   trabajáis   (same)
                   trabája   trabájan

(b) Present   trabáje   trabajémos   trabáje   trabájemos
    subjunctive   trabájes   trabajéis   trabájes   (not used)
                   trabáje   trabájen   trabáje   trabájen

In all other paradigms, stress placement is the same in the two sets of dialects.

As shown in (20), in standard dialects stress is uniformly penultimate in the present indicative and present subjunctive. In the retracting dialects, on the other hand, stress is penultimate in the present indicative but 'columnar' in the present subjunctive. In sum, in retracting dialects verb-stress placement differs from that of standard dialects in exactly one form: the first person plural of the present subjunctive. This is an absolutely minimal change in the forms of the language. No intermediate stages are possible. [23] One would expect therefore to find a corresponding minimal change in the grammar that generates these forms.

Just such a change can be found. Apparently, verb stress in retracting dialects is governed by the same principles as in standard dialects, except that instead of rule (15), retracting dialects have rule (21):

(21) $V \rightarrow [+stress] / \overline{s}]_{St} S - S \#]_{Verb}$

Illustrative derivations are given in (22):

(22)

(a) Pres subj. (retr)
   [[trabaj] e mos]
     _] S - S] (21)
     ↓
     á

(b) Pres subj. (std)
   [[trabaj___] e mos]
     *ThV] S - S] (15) not appl.
     __ - S] (13)
     ↓
     é

(c) Pres indic. (retr)
   [[trabaj + a] mos]
     * _] S-S] (21) not appl.
     __ - S] (13)
     ↓
     á

(d) Imperfect (retr)
   [[trabaj + a] ba mos]
     _] S - S] (21)
     ↓
     á

Derivation (22a) shows how rule (21) produces antepenultimate stress in the present subjunctive in retracting dialects, contrasting with penultimate stress in the corresponding forms in standard dialects (22b); (22c) shows why rule (21) does not affect present indicative forms (because only one inflectional syllable follows the stem, while (21) calls for two); and (22d) is included to show that (21) has the same effect in the imperfect in retracting dialects as (15) in standard dialects.

For convenience, (15) and (21) are repeated as (23a) and (23b), respectively:

(23) (a) $V \rightarrow [+stress]/ \begin{bmatrix} \overline{s} \\ [thV] \end{bmatrix}_{St} S - S \#]_{Vb}$ (standard)

    (b) $V \rightarrow [+stress]/ \overline{s}]_{St} S - S \#]_{Vb}$ (retracting)

The formulations in (23) reveal a very simple relationship between the verb stress rules of the two sets of dialects: standard dialects have antepenultimate stress in verbs when a two-syllable inflection follows the theme vowel; retracting dialects have discarded the theme vowel restriction.

It is not open to question that the standard rule (23a) = (15) is the historically older one (Latin had <u>amémus</u>; etc., not *<u>ámemus</u>) and thus that rule (23b) represents an innovation. This innovation is reflected in a particularly simple and extremely common type of rule change, namely, loss of part of an environment. It is a tedious but straightforward task to verify the fact that any other single change in the standard rule (23a) would have resulted in radical and highly improbable changes in the patterns of stress throughout the set of verb paradigms in Spanish. To look at the matter from a slightly different perspective, when or even if some dialect would undergo change surely could not be predicted by inspection of the set of standard rules (23a) plus (13). One can see, however, that the only change with any likelihood of occurrence much greater than zero was the one that in fact took place. This is precisely the paradigmatic change that can be associated with a minimal rule change of maximally expected type, namely, the loss of a single environmental restriction. Thus the shift in verb-stress in retracting dialects makes a very powerful case in support of the theory of language change which provides a motivation for the observation or quasi-prediction just mentioned.

Referring back to (20b) and considering the paradigmatic effect of the shift of verb-stress in retracting dialects, the stress pattern has changed from one of regular penultimate stress in standard to 'columnar' in retracting dialects. This change is strikingly reminiscent of one that occurred centuries ago in the ancestors of today's standard dialects. To put the earlier change into perspective, let us go back to the earliest relevant stage, that of Vulgar Latin. Consider the paradigms of regular conjugation <u>am</u>+<u>a</u>- 'love' given in (24):[24]

(24)

Imperfect indicative	Past subjunctive -ra- form	-sse- form
amábā amābámus	amárā amārámus	amássē amāssémus
amábās amābátis	amárās amārátis	amássēs amāssétis
amábāt amábant	amárāt amárānt	amássēt amássēnt

Future subjunctive

amáro amárĭmus
amáris amárĭtis
amárit amárint

In (24) all paradigms but the Future Subjunctive have uniform penultimate stress; the Future Subjunctive has antepenultimate stress in first and second persons plural and penultimate stress in the remaining form. These patterns, at the early date under consideration, were assigned by the 'Latin Stress Rule', which can be formulated as in (25):

$$(25) \quad V \rightarrow [\text{+stress}] \; / \; \begin{cases} \bar{S} - C_0 \breve{V} - S \;\#]_\beta \quad \text{(a)} \\ \bar{S} - S \;\#]_\beta \quad\quad\;\; \text{(b)} \\ \bar{S} \;\#]_\beta \quad\quad\quad\;\; \text{(c)} \end{cases}$$

As a result of regular and general sound changes, the paradigms in (24) were replaced in Spain by those shown in (26):[25]

(26) amába   amabámos   amára   amarámos   amásse   amassémos
        amábas amabádes   amáras amarádes   amásses amassédes
        amába   amában   amára   amáran   amásse   amássen

                       amáre   amáremos
                       amáres amáredes
                       amáre   amáren

The stress patterns in the paradigms of (26) have been inherited from those of (24). At the time of (26), however, stress could not have been assigned by the Latin Stress Rule (25) since the distinction between long and short vowels has been lost in surface representations. For example, the e of amásse/amassémos is now identical to that of amáre/amáremos, except for stress.

It seems likely that at the stage represented in (26), these para digms and others received their stress in accordance with the rules shown in (27):

$$(27) \quad V \rightarrow [\text{+stress}] \; / \; \begin{cases} \left[\begin{matrix} \bar{S} \\ [TV] \end{matrix}\right]_{St} S - S \;\#]_{Vb} \text{ in Future Subjunctive} \quad \text{(a)} \\ \\ \bar{S} - S \;\#]_\beta \quad\quad\quad\quad\quad\quad\quad\quad\quad\quad\quad\;\; \text{(b)} \\ \\ \bar{S} \;\#]_\beta \quad\quad\quad\quad\quad\quad\quad\quad\quad\quad\quad\quad\;\;\; \text{(c)} \end{cases}$$

Although the stress patterns themselves in (26) were inherited from (24), the basis on which rules operate to assign the patterns of (24)-- namely, the 'weak cluster' principle of case (a) of the Latin Stress Rule (25)--was not passed down, as was just observed, and case (a) of (25) has become morphologized as shown in (27a). In particular, antepenultimate stress is assigned to first and second person plural Future Subjunctive forms (amáremos, amáredes) not on the grounds that the stressed syllable is followed by an open syllable with a short vowel--the distinction between short and long vowels no longer being available--but rather on the basis of the morphological information shown in (27a).

The inherited stress patterns of (26) were to change shortly in some dialects of Spain, specifically the ancestors of the modern standard dialects. The paradigms that replace those of (26) are given in (28):

(28) amába amábamos   amára amáramos   amásse amássemos
amábas amábades   amáras amárades   amásses amássedes
amába amában   amára amáran   amásse amássen

amáre amáremos
amáres amáredes
amáre amáren

Now all four of the paradigms illustrated have the same pattern: stress has been retracted one syllable in the first and second persons plural of the imperfect indicative and both forms of the past subjunctive, apparently on the analogy of the future subjunctive.

The stress patterns of (28) are now the same as those of modern standard dialects (in all of which the Future Subjunctive has recently become obsolete and disappeared except for a few fixed phrases). The grammatical correlate of the shift to the stage represented in (28) is simply the loss of the morphological restriction 'in Future Subjunctive' on rule (27a). In short, rule (15) = (23a) replaces (27a), the other rules remaining the same. The parallel of this stress shift to the shift in retracting dialects discussed at the beginning of this section is as obvious as it is striking: in both cases a shift of stress in paradigms from penultimate to 'columnar' is reflected in the grammar by the loss of a morphological restriction on a rule.

One can only conclude that 'columnar' stress in paradigms is very natural, although it is difficult to see a priori why 'columnar' stress should be more natural or 'regular' than penultimate stress on every form of a paradigm. [26] And one may still ask why, if 'columnar' stress is such a nice thing, modern innovative dialects like retracting ones have not developed it in the Present Indicative? To my knowledge, there exists no tendency in any dialect, even among children, to say *trabájamos, *ámamos, and so on in the indicative. Such forms are unthinkable, even to speakers who regularly say trabájemos, ámemos, etc. in the subjunctive. Why should this be so? One particularly interesting answer is that there is no way to perform some minimal change on the rules of standard or retracting dialects so as to produce just the paradigmatic change in question (stress shifts in the indicative from, say, trabajámos to trabájamos) without violent repercussions throughout all the sets of paradigms.

Although columnar stress, as a special case of paradigm regularity, is surely natural in a reasonably clear sense, there are apparently limits on paradigmatic changes toward this natural state, limits that are imposed by the form of the rules of the grammar.

Let me attempt to formulate this suggestion more broadly. In the traditional view of linguistic change, a clear concept of synchronic grammars consisting of sets of statements or rules that apply in a certain order was generally missing, and language change was understood rather literally as change from one sound or set of sounds to another sound or set of sounds, and from one form or set of forms to another form or set of forms, and so on. One might call this the L(anguage)$_i$ > L$_{i+1}$ view.

In the 1950's a radically different view gained ground, which was based on Morris Halle's stimulating insight that, since languages are describable in terms of ordered sets of rules, the proper object of historical study is grammatical change, that is, change in the form and order of rules, rather than the direct study of the output of these rules. One might call this the G(rammar)$_i$ > G$_{i+1}$ view.

More recently, evidence has begun to accumulate that output conditions, such as the notions of paradigm regularity, opacity and transparency, conspiracies, and so on, interact with rules, and furthermore that such output conditions play a role in language change. [27] Now, if my interpretation of the historical material discussed here is on the right track, this material suggests that not only can properties of form limit changes in grammars, but also properties of grammars can limit changes in forms, in ways which are understood only meagerly at present.

APPENDIX

Hooper (1973: Chapter 3) contains statements concerning the assignment of stress to verb forms in Spanish that are considerably at variance with the proposals made in SpPh and in the present paper. It is difficult, however, to comment briefly on Hooper's interesting work in any serious way. Hooper makes it clear on virtually every page of her dissertation that she rejects generative phonological theory in the form in which it is widely known and that her intention is to argue in favor of a rival theory called Natural Generative Phonology (henceforth 'NGP'). The principal source of difficulty in assessing briefly Hooper's work on Spanish is thus that arguments that are valid in the framework of 'standard' generative phonological theory may be irrelevant in the framework of NGP, and of course conversely. For an appropriate analogy one need only recall the prohibition against 'mixing levels' in taxonomic phonological theory. Those who remember why 'mixing levels' was proscribed in most of post-Bloomfieldian

structuralism will know why this is not only not a sin in standard
generative phonology but is also not even a definable notion. Hooper
is of course keenly aware of the problem, and her criticisms of
standard generative phonology are not marred by dependence on
arguments that are valid only within her own NGP framework.

I will return immediately to the single theory-independent argument provided by Hooper for the superiority of NGP over standard
generative phonology that is based on the facts of stress patterns in
Spanish verbs. First, I must comment that it is also difficult to
evaluate Hooper's proposals on their own terms because of her failure
to come to grips with empirical data in a sufficiently explicit and
rigorous way. For example, Hooper rejects the cyclical analysis of
future and conditional forms given in SpPh. She states that 'The
evaluation of Harris' semantic argument is left to the interested
reader; suffice it to say that such a dubious relationship would not be
drawn in [NGP]. In [NGP] the future and conditional forms are analyzed as stem plus inflection' (35-36). Hooper's stress rule for these
forms is the following (40):

(29) $V \rightarrow [\text{+stress}] / \underline{\quad} \text{-r} \underline{\quad}$
         $[\text{+future}]$
      (Both future and conditional are classified as [+future].)

Hooper is no doubt justified in giving my semantic argument such
short shrift. On the other hand, that she nowhere mentions the fact
that future and conditional stems are not the same as the stems found
in any other paradigm, let alone attempts to account for this fact,
must be counted as a serious descriptive gap. Furthermore, one
searches in vain for any mention of the morphological and especially
phonological oddities of future and conditional forms (e. g. the failure
of the general glide-formation rule to apply in cases like oiré) that
are accounted for handily by the SpPh cyclical analysis.

Hooper's failure to deal with morphology is also evident in her
treatment of preterit forms. She proposes two 'alternative' rules
to assign stress to these forms (among others):

(30)
$$V \rightarrow [\text{+stress}] / \begin{bmatrix} \overline{\text{theme}} \\ \left\{ \begin{matrix} [\text{+past}] \\ [\text{-finite}] \end{matrix} \right\} \end{bmatrix} \text{(p. 39)}$$

(31) $V \rightarrow [\text{+stress}] / \begin{bmatrix} \left\{ \begin{matrix} [\text{+past}] \\ [\text{-finite}] \end{matrix} \right\} \end{bmatrix}_{\text{Verb}} + (y) \underline{\quad}$ (p. 40)
                                                                                         stem

Hooper does not explain why or how Tense-Mood-Aspect features are assigned to the Theme Vowel in (30) and to the Verb stem in (31). More important, however, is the way in which (30) or (31) actually applies to preterit forms. Hooper states that 'the stressed vowels in amé and amó are both person and number markers and theme markers' (39, emphasis in the original). No clue is given as to the morphological principles that assign such an analysis to the vowels in question. Hooper's strategy could be reconstructed as follows, with only a slight element of parody: Stress is assigned to all verb forms, including the preterit, on the X, where X is defined by unstated and apparently unconstrained morphological principles to be whatever element stress happens to fall on. One can only applaud Hooper's overall goal in attempting to articulate the foundations of NGP, namely, to devise a theory more tightly constrained than current standard generative phonology, but it is not clear to me what is gained if everything that is excluded thereby from the domain of phonology is allowed to reappear in nebulous morphological guise. In short, the difficulty with Hooper's descriptive proposals is not that they are wrong, but rather that they are formulated so inexplicitly that they cannot be evaluated in significantly more detail than has just been done.

Hooper's argument for the superiority of NGP over standard generative phonology is based on the historical data presented in section 5 of the present paper. This argument can be summarized, with some oversimplification, as follows. The NGP analysis claims that verb-stress assignment is totally morphologized, that is, the environments of the stress rules refer to morphological properties (e. g. theme vowels, tense-mood-aspect, etc.) to the total exclusion of phonological properties (penultimate syllable, etc.). On the other hand, the standard analysis, specifically that of SpPh, has both morphological and phonological conditions on its verb stress rules. Now, Hooper argues that 'before the first stress shift, the imperfect stress shift [from (26) to (28), JWH], the stress was completely penultimate on an abstract level . . . The imperfect stress shift added a complication, a special case to be included in the rule. But on the basis of the original rule there was absolutely no way to predict this development' (44). Concerning the stress shift in modern retracting dialects illustrated in (20), she continues: 'Similarly, the present tense stress shift must be regarded in [standard generative phonology] as additional complication of the rule, and this complication is also not predictable from the [standard generative phonology] rule' (44). These historical data provide evidence that the NGP analysis is correct, according to Hooper, since 'it must be the case that speakers had already analyzed stress as morphological before the two stress changes took place. This means that they were placing stress by tense/aspect <u>at the time when stress was still predictable by the penultimate stress rule</u>' (44, emphasis in the original).

The last quoted assertion is puzzling, and it is far from obvious to me what factual basis it might have. Since this is the keystone of Hooper's contentions, it should have been supported by substantive argumentation, but was not. In any event, Hooper is simply mistaken about the historical data: as illustrated in (24), (26), and (28), stress has never been 'completely penultimate' on any level at any historical stage. Hooper is of course correct in stating that the stress shift in retracting dialects must be regarded as an unexplainable 'additional complication' of the <u>SpPh</u> rule that required the identification of a morpheme manifesting imperfective aspect. But we have seen that this rule is observationally incorrect. We also have seen that on the basis of the rules proposed in the present paper--which Hooper could not have foreseen in 1973, it is only fair to add--both the ancient and the modern stress retractions can be associated with rule simplifications, and furthermore simplifications that consist of the loss of morphological restrictions.

In sum, the historical data under discussion provide no support for Hooper's claim that 'upon examining previous and on-going changes in the system, we will see that generalizations expressed in the [NGP analysis, but not those expressed in the 'standard' analysis] represent the generalizations internalized by the speakers of Spanish' (32). This claim is immune to evaluation at present in any case, since Hooper does not give even an informal statement, in NGP terms, of the stress rules for modern retracting dialects.

NOTES

1. I will not be concerned here with rules that assign levels of stress other than primary. The output of all stress rules will be written simply as [+stress] rather than [1 stress].

2. In (2) and in the rules to follow, uppercase '<u>S</u>' stands for 'syllable', and the hyphen '-' represents a syllable boundary. I have formulated rules in terms of syllables and syllable boundaries rather than in terms of segmental sequences only because I have used the expressions 'open syllable', 'closed syllable', etc. to facilitate the exposition in the text. Use of these expressions and of the symbols '<u>S</u>' and '-' is not to be interpreted as endorsement of the introduction into linguistic theory of the entities so named and symbolized. Issues are involved here that merit serious discussion--see for example Hooper (1972) and Leben (1973)--but they do not crucially affect the main points here, and I take no stand on these issues. The reader who wishes to can mentally translate all the rules into a notation referring to segmental sequences rather than to syllables.

The α in (2) is to be understood as a shorthand notation referring to all stressable categories other than verbs, e.g. nouns, adjectives, adverbs, difficult-to-classify words like sí, no, etc. I will not address the question of why certain categories are stressable (e.g. él 'he', sí 'yes') and others are not (e.g. el 'the' (masculine singular), si 'if').

3. The only exceptions I know of are obviously foreign proper names like Wáshington.

4. As one of a number of possible notational variants, [X] might be interpreted as [+rule n], where rule n is a rule identical in form to (3) but specified as a 'minor rule'.

5. For example, the shift from (old) reína 'queen' and vaína 'sheath' to (modern standard) réina, váina is due to a general process whereby high vowels contiguous to another vowel become glides with concomitant shift of stress onto the adjacent vowel. For an extensive survey of various types of stress shift see Alonso (1930:317-370).

6. The SpPh Apocope rule is given an improved formulation in Harris (1973) which does not involve the diacritic feature [D] used in SpPh. The change in the formulation of this rule has no direct consequences for the question of stress placement in nonverb forms. For fuller treatment, including discussion of exceptions to the Apocope rule, see SpPh (79 note 15; 177-183), Harris (1970), and Harris (1973).

7. Papá-type words seem to be doubly exceptional: not only do they not undergo the penultimate stress rule (2a), but also they do not undergo the word-formation rules that insert the 'gender vowels' -a, -o, -e at the end of the stems of all fully regular nouns and adjectives. (See the discussion of papél, etc.) This double exceptionality suggests a defect in our developing account of stress: one might hope to be able to account for the exceptional final stress of papá-type words on the basis of their exceptional lack of a 'gender vowel'. However, I have not been able to work out the details of any such account without running into serious obstacles.

8. It is nowhere claimed in SpPh that the diacritic feature [D] is identical to (the opposite value of) the phonological feature [tense]. In fact, the whole of SpPh section 4.2 (pp. 116-118) is devoted to precisely the argument that the identification of [D] with [tense] in a synchronic description of Spanish is totally without justification. The terms 'tense' and 'lax', however, were used in SpPh as handy but, unfortunately, misleading labels. A feature whose function is in fact diacritic rather than phonological remains the same regardless of what name it is given in imprecise locutions. There is no confusion in SpPh on this point.

9. See now Harris (1974) for fuller discussion of diphthongization.

10. For example, see Saciuk (1974).

11. With the addition of clitic pronouns, the number of unstressed syllables after the stressed one can climb as high as four; e.g. castígue+se+me+le 'let him be punished on my account', aprendiéndo+te+nos+lo '(you) learning it well for us'. Clitic pronouns, although they may form a single phonological word with a verb form, are clearly not verb forms themselves, and will be disregarded henceforth. There is brief, inconclusive discussion of several rules that convert more than one grammatical word into a single phonological word in Harris (1973).

12. Hooper (1973:37), Reyes (1972:5-7).

13. A much fuller treatment can be found in SpPh, chapters 3 and 4.

14. Trabaj- has been chosen as the sample verb because the root is long enough to illustrate various positions of stress, has no internal structure to complicate matters, and has only the vowel a, which illustrates that vowel quality is irrelevant to everything that follows.

15. The theme vowel does not appear in the surface representation of first person singular forms (trabájo) or any present subjunctive form (trabáje, etc.). In accordance with (9), the respective morphological structures are [[trabaj + a]o$_{P-N}$] and [[trabaj + a]e$_{T-M-A}$ + P-N]; the theme vowel is deleted by a morphological rule roughly of the form:

$$[[X \ V]_{St} \ V \ Y]_{Vb}$$
$$\downarrow$$
$$\emptyset$$

16. The stressed vowels in monosyllabic verb forms represent a variety of morphological elements: theme vowel (dá), present subjunctive marker (dén), person-number morpheme (dóy--y is added to monosyllabic first person singular forms in the present indicative), root vowel (hán, sál), and unclassifiable suppletive forms (és, són, sé, and perhaps vá, etc.). Thus no morphological condition must or can be placed on the stress rule for monosyllabic verbs, as is also the case with rule (12).

17. In casual speech the second person plural person-number ending is phonetically [-ys]. For evidence that a more abstract representation of this morpheme is in fact -is, and hence that the second person plural forms in (14) are in fact stressed on the antepenultimate vowel, see Harris (1973).

18. This flaw was not caught in SpPh because second person plural forms were excluded from consideration, and it has not been noticed by any critic of SpPh.

19. See the discussion of (8) above.

20. Note in particular that the sole peculiarity in the abstract representation of the forms of irregular pod-, namely, absence of the theme vowel, accounts automatically and simultaneously for the three idiosyncratic properties shared by the surface representations of all irregular preterits: (a) penultimate stress, (b) first person singular e rather than regular í, (c) third person singular o rather than regular ió.

21. Brame and Bordelois (1973) criticize the SpPh account of preterit forms—on rather weak grounds, it seems to me. But whatever force this criticism may have had, it is less applicable to the somewhat revised account sketched. In any event, Brame and Bordelois do not come to grips with the full range of data and they offer no alternative. They state: 'We have not investigated the past tense conjugations in sufficient detail to warrant further discussion of how forms such as un[yó] or com[yó], are to be handled . . .' (p. 162, footnote). Certain proposals of Hooper (1973) are discussed briefly in the Appendix to the present paper.

22. For information on the geographical distribution of 'retracting' dialects see Alonso (1930:345-349).

23. In the Latin American retracting dialects under consideration, the second and third conjugations (e- and i-stems, respectively) have the same stress patterns as the first conjugation (a-stems) verb illustrated in (20). Mondéjar (1970) discusses Andalusian dialects whose verb stress patterns are like standard dialects in the first conjugation but like Latin American retracting dialects in the second and third. Thus the Andalusian dialects might at first glance seem to constitute an intermediate stage between standard and retracting Latin American dialects. There is no evidence, however, that the Andalusian dialects are in fact genealogically intermediate. Just the opposite is the case: retracted verb stress is not found in precisely those American dialects that are generally believed to have been most influenced by Andalusian Spanish, but is found in dialects for which Andalusian influence is believed to be minimal or nonexistent, e.g. in Peru, Chile, Argentina, Paraguay, Uruguay, and highland Mexico.

24. For convenience, the paradigms in (24) are identified not by their function in Vulgar Latin but rather by their function in premodern Spanish.

25. The chronology and other details of consonant and vowel changes between (24) and (26) are not strictly relevant to the main topic, namely the assignment of stress in verb forms. Detailed information on all of these topics can be found in a number of handbooks, for example Menéndez Pidal (1962:268-313).

26. For discussion of the notion of 'paradigm regularity' see King (1972, 1973), and Kiparsky (1971).

27. In addition to the references in note 26, see also Kiparksy (1973) and Malkiel (1968).

REFERENCES

Alonso, A. 1930. Problemas de dialectología hispanoamericana. In: A. M. Espinosa. Estudios sobre el español de Nuevo Méjico, Parte I. Buenos Aires, Facultad de Filosofía y Letras de la Universidad de Buenos Aires.

Brame, M. K. and I. Bordelois. 1973. Vocalic alternations in Spanish. Linguistic Inquiry 4:111-168.

Harris, J. W. 1969. Spanish phonology. Cambridge, Mass., MIT Press.

_____. 1970. A note on Spanish plural formation. Lg. 46:928-930.

_____. 1973. Las formas verbales de segunda persona plural y otras cuestiones de fonología y morfología. Revista de Lingüística Aplicada y Teórica. 11:31-60. Universidad de Concepción, Chile.

_____. 1974. Morphologication of phonological rules: An example from Chicano Spanish. In: Linguistic studies in Romance Languages. Ed. by R. J. Campbell, M. G. Goldin, and M. C. Wang. Washington, D.C., Georgetown University Press.

Hooper, J. B. 1972. The syllable in phonological theory. Lg. 48: 525-540.

_____. 1973. Aspects of natural generative phonology. Unpublished doctoral dissertation, UCLA.

King, R. D. 1972. A note on opacity and paradigm regularity. Linguistic Inquiry 3:535-539.

_____. 1973. Rule insertion. Lg. 49:551-578.

Kiparsky, P. 1971. Historical linguistics. In: A survey of linguistic science. Ed. by W. O. Dingwall. College Park, Linguistics Program, University of Maryland.

_____. 1973. Abstractness, opacity, and global rules. Indiana University Linguistics Club.

Leben, W. R. 1973. Suprasegmental phonology. Unpublished doctoral dissertation, MIT.

Malkiel, Y. 1968. The inflectional paradigm as an occasional determinant of sound change. In: Directions for historical linguistics. Ed. by W. P. Lehmann and Y. Malkiel. Austin, University of Texas Press.

Menéndez Pidal, R. 1962. Manual de gramática histórica española. Madrid, Espasa-Calpe.

Mondéjar, J. 1970. El verbo andaluz: Formas y estructuras. Supplement to Revista de filología española. Vol. 90, Madrid.

Reyes, R. 1972. Studies in Chicano Spanish. Unfinished doctoral dissertation, Harvard University.

Saciuk, B. 1974. Spanish stress and language change. In: Linguistic studies in Romance Languages. Ed. by R. J. Campbell, M. G. Goldin, and M. C. Wang. Washington, D.C., Georgetown University Press.

SPANISH TÚ AND USTED: PATTERNS OF INTERCHANGE

GARY D. KELLER

The City College of the City University of New York

Over the last two years I have been conducting a series of investigations on the symmetrical and asymmetrical interchange of tú and usted
among native Spanish speakers in New York City and Mexico City. [1]
My research has made use primarily of self-rating questionnaires,
but I have also done substantial field investigations. For example, I
have enlisted the aid of shopkeepers, school crossing guards,
teachers, etc. to question children or adolescents in a manner pertinent to tú or usted responses. With very young children and early
schoolchildren I have been making use of what might be called a
'bilingual paradigm' where the parent or teacher puts on a very brief
skit in English between, say, a grandparent and a child or a police-
man and a child. The child then replays (e.g. translates) the skit in
Spanish for a second child. Since the English material invariably
involves the pronoun 'you', the act of translation implicitly confronts
the child with a tú/usted option.

The sample groups with which I have conducted my investigations
are the following: (1) New York City children in elementary school
grades 1-6, (2) New York City adolescents at puberty (with a median
age of 14 years), (3) Spanish-speaking adults in New York City, (4)
New York City adults who have entered compadrazgo relationships,
(5) Mexico City adults who have experienced compadrazgo relationships.

In addition, I am now conducting a longitudinal study with very
young (preschool) children in an effort to map the onset of patterns
of tú and usted usage.

These studies have generated an extensive amount of data. I have been correlating the use of tú/usted with the obvious variables such as age, sex, socioeconomic level, years of education, country or region of origin; and with some less obvious variables such as years of residence in the United States, proficiency in English, frequency of usage of such titles as don and doña, and phonological data such as the pronunciation of compadre/comadre as compadre/comadre or as compai/comai. Not all of the data has yet been completely assimilated and analyzed. Therefore, at this time I will confine myself to the presentation of three rather striking aspects of my research: (1) the developmental pattern of nonreciprocal usted usage in the Spanish speaker; (2) the relationship between compadrazgo and pronominal mode of address; (3) the relationship between the English 'omnibus' pronoun, you, and tú and usted in New York City Spanish.

1. The developmental pattern of nonreciprocal usted usage in the Spanish speaker

I am referring to the phenomenon where the subject under investigation uses usted with another interlocutor but receives tú rather than usted in return. This type of nonreciprocal usage is productively explained by reference to the power and solidarity norms that operate in society and which affect all sorts of modes of address. Without going into an extended treatment of these norms, which would be beyond the scope of this paper, [2] I will note that nonreciprocal usted usage is a linguistic index of a superordinate/subordinate relationship which may be based on a number of considerations such as relative prestige or status, relative age or social distance, or relative socioeconomic level between interlocutors.

On the basis of my investigations with children, adolescents, and adults I am hypothesizing that the use of nonreciprocal usted as a function of age may be plotted according to the curve described in Figure 1.

The ordinate of the function plotted on Figure 1, frequency of nonreciprocal usted (%), has been computed by measuring the mean percentage difference between usted sent and usted received for the following relationships between experimental subject and interlocutor: mother, father, grandfather, grandmother, teacher, aunt or uncle, and clergyman. It should be noted that not all subject-interlocutor categories on which I gathered data are included in the index of frequency of nonreciprocal usted. Data gathered on friends and on older and younger siblings of both sexes indicated very little nonreciprocal usted with these interlocutors. The norm for children, adolescents, and adults alike is mutual tú. Therefore to include these categories would only serve to fudge the index. On the other

FIGURE 1. Hypothesized relationship between relative frequency
of nonreciprocal <u>usted</u> and chronological age

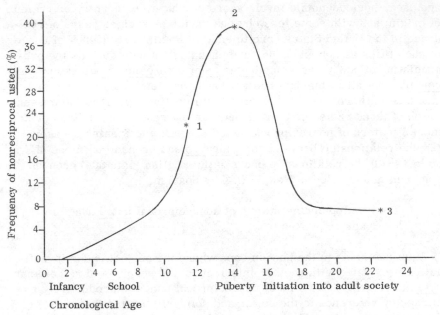

hand, wide variations were registered between adolescents and
adults for the following two categories: person working in a store
and stranger on the street.   The tendency was for adolescents to
register a net nonreciprocal <u>usted</u> in terms of their pronoun usage
while adults registered a net <u>expectation</u> of nonreciprocal <u>usted</u> on
the part of the interlocutor.   I suspect that the categories in question
were too vague and therefore elicited different entities for different
age groups.   Perhaps adolescents conceived of employees and
strangers as respectable or worthy of deference while adults en-
visioned them as shabby or beneath them.   At any rate these two
ill-defined categories were excluded from the index; nevertheless,
they are referred to in connection with differences in usage based on
sex.

Figure 1 is a hypothetical function but it is supported by the three
experimental studies that I have performed thus far.   These three
studies constitute the basis for the plotting of the curve and in Figure 1
are marked by asterisks and numerals.   The studies are the following: (1) a sample of 88 New York City elementary schoolchildren
with a median age of 11 years, 7 months; (2) a sample of 100 New
York City adolescent schoolchildren with a median age of 14 years;
(3) a sample of 100 New York City college evening students and
graduate students with a median age of 22 years, 6 months.

Subjects (or their parents) came from numerous parts of Latin America, but with the vast majority either from Puerto Rico or the Dominican Republic. The investigator was not able to detect signifi- cant differences in tú/usted usage between Puerto Ricans and Domini- cans. The numbers of subjects of other nationalities were too small to permit an evaluation of such differences. However, the handful of Cubans in the sample appeared to be less inclined toward nonrecipro- cal usted usage than the norm. It would be worthwhile in future in- vestigations to attempt a systematic comparison between Cubans and other nationalities. However, this tendency might not be related to nationality as much as to socioeconomic level. Almost all of the sub- jects in my three studies were of low or lower middle class socio- economic class (as measured by two factors, description of father's and/or mother's employment, and years formal education of father and/or mother). Among the few Cuban subjects there were more middle class individuals. Almost all of the subjects were Spanish- English bilinguals; but all subjects were native Spanish speakers. The average residence in the United States for each group was the following: (1) elementary schoolchildren, 3 years, 1 month; (2) adolescent schoolchildren, 3 years, 4 months; (3) adult college stu- dents, 6 years, 5 months. As indicated in Figure 1 the composite frequency of nonreciprocal usted for each group was the following:

Group 1, Elementary Schoolchildren: 22%
Group 2, Adolescent Schoolchildren: 38.8%
Group 3, Adult College Students: 6.8%

These composites may be broken down into actual subject-inter- locutor categories:

		Children	Adolescents	Adults
Mother:	% usted sent	12	49	10
	% usted received	5	13	6
	% difference	7	36	4
Father:	% usted sent	17	48	12
	% usted received	5	14	7
	% difference	12	34	5
Grandfather:	% usted sent	55	77	48
	% usted received	20	26	31
	% difference	35	51	17

		Children	Adolescents	Adults
Grandmother:	% usted sent	41	70	41
	% usted received	15	26	33
	% difference	26	44	8
Teacher:	% usted sent	70	90	94
	% usted received	26	39	89
	% difference	44	51	5
Aunt or Uncle:	% usted sent	20	46	28
	% usted received	8	24	21
	% difference	12	22	7
Clergyman:	% usted sent	66	96	96
	% usted received	48	62	94
	% difference	18	34	2
Total mean difference %:		22	38.8	6.8

The other two studies that I am acquainted with that are pertinent here also tend to support the hypothesized function in Figure 1. Marín (1972), surveying adult Spanish speakers in Canada, arrived at results similar to mine with the New York City adult sample. However, since Marín's survey measured only the relative frequency of the subject's tú and usted usage, but not the relative frequency of tú and usted which the subject received from others, his data cannot be plotted according to the index in Figure 1. Lambert (1967) tested 136 French Canadian adolescent boys with results similar to my adolescent group. A reanalysis of Lambert's data, which was reported strictly in frequencies, yields the following breakdown (note that subject-interlocutor categories are slightly different):

	% Vous sent	% Vous received	% Difference
Mother	48	4	44
Parents	49	5	44
Grandparents	79	10	69
Aunts, Uncles	77	10	67
Teachers	98	94	4
Priests	98	70	28
Nuns	92	85	7
Older people	87	25	62
Strangers	97	81	16
Total mean difference			37.9%

There are significant differences between the Lambert sample and my New York City adolescent sample, not only among specific subject-interlocutor categories (e.g. teacher) but also in terms of the variables of socioeconomic class, age (Lambert's group ranged from 16-19 years), sex of subject, and of course, the language of the subject: French versus Spanish. Nevertheless, the high frequency of nonreciprocal vous usage (37.9%) would appear to indicate that French Canadian adolescents experience the same sort of behavioral expectations and linguistic tensions as New York City Spanish-speaking adolescents. On the basis of such findings it is at least conceivable to begin speculating about a general feature similar to that plotted on Figure 1 for languages which code different personal pronouns on the basis of intimacy/distance. I should note that Lambert found (1967: 616) a significant relationship between socioeconomic class and usage. 'The children from professional, white-collar, and blue-collar backgrounds, respectively, used tú and vous with their parents in the following ratios: 13:2; 23:15; and 22:38 . . .'

If the representation indicated in Figure 1 holds as accurate in the light of ongoing and future investigations, then one might conclude that in childhood and the onset of adolescence, nonreciprocal usted is a linguistic index of 'maturity'--its linguistic expectation is associated with behavioral expectations about the child's or adolescent's sense of responsibility, deference, and awareness of social decorum.

On the other hand, with the approach of adulthood, decreased nonreciprocal usted becomes the linguistic index of 'maturity'; the late adolescent and young adult is increasingly accepted (in terms of both social situations and ongoing relationships between interlocutors) as a member of a solidary adult society. As is characteristic in other behavioral domains, the linguistic and social tension inherent in nonreciprocal tú/usted usage falls most heavily on the adolescent who is expected to be mature enough to respect social decorum, to rank himself or herself appropriately under his or her elders, but who is not expected to be so 'mature' or 'disrespectful' as to merit a mutual tú (or mutual usted) relationship.

As the curve indicates and as empirical research has confirmed, adult sons and daughters register markedly less nonreciprocal usted than do pubertal adolescents in all categories used to compile the index. Also, adults are more likely to use mutual tú with immediate superordinates or strangers than adolescents or children. An adult will usually have a mutual tú relationship with his immediate boss, say in a factory or office, and will relate on a mutual usted basis with a substantial superior. Of course, we should note that the variety of social situations is much more expanded for the adult than for the adolescent. Thus while pubertal adolescents establish invariant pronoun usage with a given interlocutor, this is not necessarily

the case of the adult or late adolescent. For example, one can find
numerous cases where college or even high school students will use
tú with their teachers in all situations except the classroom where
they revert to usted. In general, adults are more likely than adolescents or children to expand the spectrum of social situations in
accordance with a mutual tú pragmatic--that is, they are more likely
to interpret casual social situations in such a way that mutual tú (rather
than mutual usted or asymmetrical tú/usted interchanges) may be used.

In Figure 1 the extreme left of the curve predicts that nonreciprocal
usted will increase gradually over childhood. Preliminary results of
a longitudinal study of preschool children that I am undertaking indicate
that the baby's language use is marked exclusively by mutual tú. Tú
is acquired first, usted appears to reflect social demand characteristics, particularly with the onset of schooling. Interviews with
mothers record that parents have compelled usted from their 2-, 3-,
and 4-year-old children in social situations where their children's
use of tú seemed embarrassing to them. This type of situation is
easy enough to conceive. For example, a generous or sagacious
storeowner gives a candy to the child whenever he or she comes in.
At some time the mother forces the child to change his or her,
¡ Dame un dulce! to Por favor, don Catarino, ¿puede usted darme un
dulce? These reports of embarrassment-compulsion instances support my contention that increased nonreciprocal usted is a linguistic
index of maturity up to and including puberty.

The effect of socialization leading to increased usted usage is
markedly reinforced by formal schooling. Preliminary results indicate that in New York City, the elementary school environment is a
major factor in the patterning of usted usage. Children appear to use
usted with their teachers (and generalize semantically to other adults)
in those school environments where it is demanded of them. This
fact is hit home in a striking manner by the following experience. I
found that in one school which has both a bilingual program and a
monolingual English program, Spanish-speaking first, second, and
third graders in the bilingual program used usted with teachers and
other elders because it was demanded of them; but Spanish-speaking
elementary school children in the monolingual English program
rarely used usted at all.

In addition to the trends plotted in Figure 1, there are significant
sex differences in pronoun usage among adolescents. In the sample
53% of the adolescent boys used usted with their mothers while only
43% adolescent girls did so. On the other hand, 21% adolescent boys
received usted from their fathers while only 7% girls did so. With
respect to persons working in a store, 19% adolescent boys used tú
while only 6% adolescent girls did so. With respect to strangers on
the street the percentages were, respectively, 12% and 2%.

Conversely, boys received 63% and 41% tú, respectively, from persons working in a store and strangers on the street, while for girls the comparable percentages were 34% and 17%.

The last set of statistics is understandable enough. Girls would use usted as a self-protective device with strangers on the street or employees in a store, and this pragmatic is responded to in kind by employees and strangers. The solidarity norm is advancing in the Hispanic world but not so much as to permit casual heterosexual exchanges of tú on the street. However, it is difficult to theorize why sons are using usted more with their mothers than do daughters; why fathers use usted more with daughters than with sons. Is this an index of relative heterosexual distance or even alienation within the nuclear family? Clearly, a great deal more research in the general area of pronoun usage with respect to sex differences and socioeconomic and age differences must be performed before these questions can be answered.

A comparison of the three samples shows that usted usage with respect to grandfather versus grandmother varies systematically. The percentages for children, adolescents, and adults, respectively, for grandfather versus grandmother are: 35% versus 26%; 51% versus 44%, and 17% versus 8%. These systematic differences are what we would expect inasmuch as in Hispanic culture the grandfather is a more dominant, authoritative, and distant figure than the grandmother.

In sum, the curve that I have hypothesized in Figure 1 reflecting nonreciprocal usted usage as a function of chronological age, while certainly in need of further reinforcing studies, does have a body of empirical data that support it--nor do I know of any data which run contrary to its predictions. However, certain qualifications must be made. First, the data, with the exception of observations and parent interviews of very young children, are based on self-rating scales and questionnaires. One cannot be sure of the amount of distortion from true usage these artifacts produce. An actual field investigation of discourse between experimental subjects and interlocutors would be highly desirable in order to promote corroboration. This would be an expensive and extremely arduous undertaking. Second, we need to investigate the effect of socioeconomic level more. Lambert's study exposed a very strong relation between socioeconomic background and the form of address the subject used. Moreover, Brown and Gilman's theory, pointing to T and V usage as indices of power and solidarity norms, is substantially based on socioeconomic considerations. It is important to recall that all three of my samples use preponderantly low class and lower middle class subjects. One might expect somewhat different results in the direction of less nonreciprocal usted for subjects (or subjects' parents) in higher income brackets and/or more years of formal schooling. Third, these studies demand replication in another Spanish-speaking area, preferably in a low English contact area so that the question of potentially confounding variables such as the influence of English or transculturation may be put to rest.

2. The relationship between compadrazgo and pronominal mode of address

My results in this area are based on two concurrent studies, one with 100 individuals of Puerto Rican, Dominican, Cuban, and other extraction residing in New York, representing 261 compadrazgo relationships; the other with 112 subjects living in a barriada of Mexico City embodying 297 compadrazgo relationships. Since the findings are consonant with each other (I detect no significant differences based on national origin) I will report both studies as one. I must make some significant qualifications before presenting the main results. Pronoun usage and compadrazgo is a very complicated affair. A subject is likely to have more than one compadre or comadre and not all subjects treat all compadres alike, at least in mode of address. The same subject may use tú with one compadre and usted with another. This reflects the reasons behind compadre selection in the first place. For example, a worker in a factory, for his first child--a son--may seek out a powerful acquaintance as a compadre for reasons of security. With the second child, a daughter, he may select a childhood buddy as compadre, as one subject put it, no más porque somos meros cuates. Another important complication is that women tend to designate relatives as comadres to a greater degree than men designate relatives as compadres. Men tend to turn cuates or panas into compadres. For the benefit of anyone unacquainted with these terms, cuate is a Mexican and Chicano designation for an intimate friend, pana is the Puerto Rican equivalent for the same concept. Moreover, cuate and pana are terms almost exclusively in the male domain; I have never heard of a woman refer to her cuate[3] and only very rarely has a woman admitted to panas. The fact that women tend to select relatives, particularly sisters, as comadres helps explain the sex differences in my pronoun results. One final qualification: the existence of a compadrazgo does not insure that a subject will use the designation compadre/comadre. Of our total sample 32% called their compadres/comadres only by name. Of this group women outnumbered men approximately 2 to 1. Once again, this would seem to indicate that the compadrazgo institution is male-oriented. Of the total sample 2% used don or doña and the name to refer to compadres or comadres.

The results of my investigations are the following:

(1) Of the total sample of individuals 78% used tú or usted uniformly with all compadres/comadres. Of those who distinguished between compadres/comadres, using tú for one and usted for other(s), women outnumbered men by approximately 2 to 1.

(2) Of the total 558 compadrazgo relationships, 31% maintained mutual tú before and after compadrazgo; 42% maintained mutual usted before and after compadrazgo; 27% reflected a change from tú to usted as a result of compadrazgo. Therefore compadrazgo is indexed by usted for 69% or over two-thirds of the sample.

(3) Since 27% of the sample reflected a change from tú to usted, we are able to conclude that there is a significant tendency both in New York City and Mexico City for adults who have progressed from a cuate, pana, or other, undesignated intimate relationship, to mark this passage by a linguistic change from mutual tú to mutual usted. The overwhelming reasons for explaining this change on the part of the subjects were because: 'compadrazgo is a sacred relationship and implies great responsibilities', 'compadrazgo is a serious and formal relationship', 'compadres demand mutual respect'. I found only one case where a subject progressed from an usted to a tú relationship.

(4) There was a significant sex difference with respect to changes from tú to usted. Of the total number of individuals who performed such changes 59% were men and 41% were women. Recall again that there was a larger number of sisters who functioned as comadres than brothers who took on the role of compadres. Changes from tú to usted are not registered with respect to sibling compadres or comadres.

(5) There were the expected differences on the basis of socio-economic class, age, and level of education. I should note that my sample only distinguishes between low socioeconomic class and lower middle class. The low class subjects used more usted with their compadres than the lower middle class. Of the total sample of 558 compadrazgo relationships, 196 were maintained by lower middle class subjects and 362 were maintained by low class subjects. Of the lower middle class subsample, 78 (40%) were maintained with tú before and after compadrazgo. Of the lower class subsample, 95 (26%) were maintained with tú before and after compadrazgo; 153 (43%) were maintained with usted; and 114 (31%) changed from tú to usted with the onset of compadrazgo.

The same tendency is obtained, respectively, with older subjects versus younger subjects, and fewer years of formal schooling versus more years of formal schooling. Of the total number of individuals, 54 changed from tú to usted. Of these 54 individuals, 21 (38%) were between ages 20-40 years; 28 (53%) were between 40-60; and 5 (9%)

were 60 or over. The relationship between age and pronoun usage
may be seen in another light. Of the total sample of 212 individuals,
119 were between 20-40; 82 individuals were between 40-60; and 11
were over 60. Therefore, of the subsample of 20-40 year olds, 18%
changed from tú to usted; of the subsample of 40-60 year olds, 34%
changed from tú to usted; and of the subsample of 60 or over, 45%
changed from tú to usted.

Similarly, with respect to formal schooling, of the total number
of individuals who changed from tú to usted, 34 (63%) had a primary
education or less, 14 (26%) had 7-10 years of formal schooling; 4 (7%)
had 11-12 years of formal schooling; and 2 (4%) had over 12 years.
Of the total sample of 212 individuals, 112 had a primary education
or less, 50 had 7-10 years formal schooling, 40 had 11-12 years,
and 10 had over 12 years formal schooling. Therefore, of the subsample of primary education or less, 30% changed from tú to usted;
of the 7-10 years formal schooling group, 28% changed from tú to
usted, of the 11-12 years formal school group, 10% changed from tú
to usted, and among those with over 12 years, 20% changed from tú
to usted.

These types of differences with respect to socioeconomic class,
age, and level of education are typically obtained in this field of investigation, not only in Spanish, but also with other languages that
encode different pronominal modes of address based on levels of
intimacy/distance.

3. The relationship between the English 'omnibus' pronoun, you,
   and tú and usted in New York City Spanish

I am concerned here with the possible influence of English you on
Spanish usage in New York City, where the potential for English influence is substantial. It should be noted that the English 'omnibus'
pronoun, you, under pertinent circumstances may be translated by
Spanish tú, usted, ustedes, vosotros, vosotras, ti, te, os, lo, la,
le, los, las, les, se, and vos. In light of the singularity of the English pronoun versus the multiplicity in Spanish, one might expect that
if English usage were to affect Spanish in New York City, it would be
in such a way as to reduce usted usage and expand tú usage.

It is not certain what general effect English you might have on tú
and usted in New York City (or other English contact areas) but preliminary evidence indicates that such an effect is minimal or nonexistent. The data gathered from the New York City adolescent
sample used exclusively Spanish-English bilinguals with a mean of
three years, four months residence in the United States. All indi-
cations are that the traditional forms for tú and usted usage are still
very much in effect for these adolescents. On the other hand, I have

noted the virtual lack of usted among certain early elementary schoolchildren. Nevertheless, one cannot tell whether this is due to English language contact, some other variable such as systematic changes
in cultural values, or if it is characteristic of children's Spanish in
the Hispanic world generally. In order to answer these questions one
must conduct further studies directly comparing the onset and maintenance of tú/usted usage patterns between Spanish-speaking regions
characterized by high English contact versus those experiencing low
English language contact. However, I should recall that in at least
one school I surveyed which had both a bilingual and monolingual
English program, the Spanish-surnamed children in the bilingual
program used usted with regularity, while the Spanish-surnamed
children in the monolingual program almost never used this pronoun.
This phenomenon would seem to point to the significant, perhaps even
critical impairment of certain developmental Spanish language skills--
particularly in the area of pragmatics--among Spanish-surnamed children in monolingual English programs. Similarly, this fact argues
strongly for the desirability and benefits of Spanish-English bilingual
programs for Spanish-speaking youngsters.

With respect to very young children I have noted a tendency to use
tú as a disjunctive pronoun instead of ti (with the exception of contigo
which is more common than contugo). Thus one often hears, No voy
sin tú or antes de tú, después de tú, etc. It is very dubious that this
phenomenon has anything to do with English. More likely it is the
product of analogical leveling comparable to the child's production of
sabo or sepo instead of sé. Though it is a minor point, it would be
enlightening to observe its existence in low English contact areas
once linguists get around to investigating the almost totally virgin
territory of Spanish developmental psycholinguistics.

NOTES

1. The author wishes to thank Ana Zentella, Gloria Castelluccio,
and Rafael Núñez, graduate students at New York University who
participated in the data gathering and preliminary analysis of the New
York City compadrazgo sample. Acknowledgments are also in order
for the students in the Seminar on Research Methods in Spanish/
English Bilingualism at The City College of the City University of
New York for their aid in developing research materials for very
young children.

2. For a general treatment of the power and solidarity norms,
see Brown and Gilman (1960) and Brown (1965); for a specific application to the Spanish language, Keller (1974). Ford (1974) pretends
to build upon and rectify Brown and Gilman's theory. This article
is useful for its observations (unfortunately, unquantified) of tu and

vous usage in France as a consequence of the political unrest of 1968;
but the author's failure to adequately distinguish between actual pronouns and pronominal norms as well as his ignorance of the theoretical material in Brown (1965) leads him astray in his criticism of
Brown and Gilman.

3. I am indebted to Giorgio Perissinotto for his observations
that on rare occasions women will use cuatacha or even cuata.

REFERENCES

Brown, Roger. 1965. Social psychology. New York, The Free
    Press.
Brown, Roger and Albert Gilman. 1960. The pronouns of power and
    solidarity. In: Style in language. Ed. by Thomas A. Sebeok.
    Cambridge, The Technology Press of Massachusetts Institute of
    Technology.
Ford, Jerome C. 1974. The semantics of direct address pronouns
    in French. The French Review 47. 1143-57.
Keller, Gary D. 1974. La norma de solidaridad y la de poder en los
    pronombres de tratamiento: un bosquejo diacrónico y una
    investigación del español de Nueva York. The Bilingual Review/
    La revista bilingüe 1. 42-58.
Lambert, W. E. 1967. The use of tu and vous as forms of address
    in French Canada: A pilot study. Journal of Verbal Learning and
    Verbal Behavior 6. 614-17.
Marín, Diego. 1972. El uso de 'Tú' y 'usted' en el español actual.
    Hispania 55. 904-08.

SET THEORY AND THE REFERENTS
OF SPANISH VERBS

JACQUELINE M. KIRAITHE
California State University, Fullerton

CARMEN SÁNCHEZ SADEK
University of Southern California

Abstract. This paper is based on a study (Thornton 1971) which makes a tentative classification, in selected sets, of the referents of some Spanish verbs, working with other concomitant factors, and which tries to discover from this classification what may be revealed about the semantic and syntactic potentials of those verbs which are members of each set. It is an investigation of what may be learned not about Spanish verbs as surface features of the language, nor their overt structural features, but rather about their referents and the structures in which they are found--that is, the relationship between a formalistic classification and a referential classification.

If all events were classified in sets according to given criteria, what could be learned about how Spanish culture perceives certain distinctions and about how this perception is reflected in the linguistic organization of reality? In order to answer that question, it is necessary to determine if there is any productive method for the organization, in sets, of those events which are described in speech by structural forms marked 'verb'.

This paper is based on a study (Thornton 1971) which attempted to answer the above question by making a tentative classification, in selected sets, of the referents of some Spanish verbs, working with other concomitant factors, and to discover from this classification what may be revealed about the semantic and syntactic potentials

of those verbs which are members of each set. It is an investigation
of what may be learned not about the verbs as surface features of the
language, nor their overt structural features such as suffixes, but
rather about their referents and the structures in which they are
found--that is, the relationship between a formalistic classification
and a referential classification.

A basic assumption is that semantic sets of verb labels interact
with other sets in order to generate logical meaning, according to the
formula:

Label (name of action) + function + combinatory potential
= Meaning.

Earlier linguistic theories tended to deemphasize semantic meaning as a factor in linguistic analysis, leaving the discussion to
semanticists and philologists, and placing more importance on that
type of meaning displayed by morphological forms and overt markings
than on the base meanings of labels for referents in objective reality.
Current linguists, however, among them Bull (1965), Chafe (1971),
Katz and Postal (1964), and McCawley (1968), now indicate the need
for semantic description as an integral element of a complete linguistic description of a language. This present study demonstrates
that semantic meaning is essential to complete understanding of the
Spanish linguistic organization of reality.

Since verbs are not marked morphologically for sets as are entity
labels (Bergen 1971), and because verb labels ordinarily represent a
concatenation of events, the classification must be made on the basis
of an especially predominant and distinguishing feature of the event,
such as a description of movement. This criterion does not involve
a sophisticated level of comprehension, as evidenced by the fact that
the average native speaker is capable of hearing most new verb
labels and automatically assigning them to appropriate sets, subsequently understanding and formulating new utterances. 'Set theory'
differs from transformational 'performance-competence' theory by
recognizing that speakers must classify at a precoding level before
properly encoding messages. Deep structure cannot be determined
by analyzing encoded messages, since alternative forms may include
multiple isolated segments as in chancletear--andar haciendo mucho
ruido con las chancletas (chancletear 'to go about clattering one's
slippers').

Most Spanish verbs have multiple referents. Seeing or hearing a
label in combination with different sets of subjects and objects and/
or sentence completions helps to define meaning in that occurrence.
Thus, people + comer = 'to eat'; people + comer + context of games
= 'to win'; light + comer = 'to fade'; chemicals + comer = 'to corrode',

etc. Just as set theory defines meaning for individual verbs, it operates for sets of verb labels. When the same label appears in several sets, its meaning in each is defined by the interacting sets.

What establishes that the sets are neither accidental nor random, nor merely products of available options in the language, is that any members of a given set may be transformed or reformulated in the same construction(s) as may all other members of the set, displaying an underlying logic in organization. As an example, all of the members of one subset of the set 'be' (so named because it encompasses ser, estar, hacer, tener, haber) can be restated as ser + noun: abogadear--ser un abogado malo o engañoso, piratear--ser pirata, bribonear--ser bribón, etc. The system generates a verb from a noun base, and since the referent of the noun is a member of a certain set, then all verbs generated from an underlying entity set are members of the same set. Similarly, adjectives derived from an underlying entity set are members of the same set.

Although substantial cultural information is disclosed when terminology is divided by microglossaries, i. e. verbs relating to animals, to medicine, to religion, to agriculture, etc., structural information is derived only from subsets which are described by observing specific critical features in reality.

For example, if the microglossary 'Agriculture' is viewed, two major subdivisions become immediately apparent: (A) activities in which humans deal with agriculture, and (B) activities of growth and decay in which plants have the grammatical role of subject-doer. Under (A), there are six subsets: (1) preparation of land, (2) planting and sowing, (3) care of growing plants and surrounding earth, (4) harvesting and post-harvesting activities, (5) activities related to the production of specialized agricultural products, and (6) storage of agricultural products.

All of the verbs in these subsets describe activities which can only be performed by humans. They are potentially transitive, although they do not require objects in order to generate the given meanings (Thornton 1971:87-88). If an object is stated, it will belong to the sets of 'growing things', 'land', or 'agricultural products'. It is important to reiterate, however, that it is the interaction of these 'sets' which produces meaning.

Just as the nature of the subject may be specified by the nature of the event, so may the nature of the direct object. Unless one is speaking metaphorically, people do not 'throw rain' or 'caress flour', etc.

Other differences in the Spanish linguistic organization of reality may be seen in that there are descriptions of functions which must be limited by choice of the appropriate symbol for the referent in Spanish, although they are not in English, as demonstrated below. Plants, humans, animals, and inanimate objects may all change, get old, or acquire some attribute. English most frequently makes the choice of symbol to describe these occurrences through the choice of nouns, whereas Spanish embeds specialized meanings in verb symbols. The differences noted are, at least to this degree, morphological. However, Spanish also contains cover terms as well as specialized verb symbols to describe how each of the categories of entities performs these activities. For example:

The cat gets sick.	El gato se enferma.
The man gets sick.	El hombre se enferma.
The horses get sick.	Los caballos se enferman.
The cattle get sick.	El ganado se enferma.

In this case, the choice of symbol--a cover term--is parallel in Spanish and English for all subjects. However, when 'getting sick' is limited to specific illnesses for cats, horses, cattle, and men, specialized terminology is generated because of differences in reality which relate to the entity chosen as subject.

The cat gets sick from eating mice.
El gato se enratona.

The man gets indigestion (sick from an eating habit).
El hombre se indigesta.

The horses get sick from (eating) too much feed and water.
Los caballos se encebadan.

The cattle get sick from (eating) too much salt.
El ganado se salmuera.

The sets of men, cats, horses, and cattle all interact with enfermarse; only the set of cats interacts with enratonarse; only horses or cattle may interact with encebadarse and salmuerarse. The difference between these sets of animate entities shown here is in their eating habits; this is reflected in the linguistic organization and the generation of appropriate verbs.

When sets are established by specific criteria, the basic one is that there be a critical feature shared by all members. Members of another set do not share the primary distinguishing feature. On the surface level, all members included in the original study are classified lexically as verbs. Therefore, the basic criteria are first, that an event be described by a verb, and second, that the event be of a certain kind, characterized by some especially distinguishing feature which is shared by all other members of the same set. A symbol for movement, whether one, two, or three dimensional, or whether it be of animals, humans, or liquids, for example, would belong to the same set as all other verbs which described movement. Within the cover sets, subsets are established according to other, more refined categorizations based on more specific and limiting characteristics, whenever this seems to be significant.

The establishment of such sets should reveal a logical and meaningful grammatical consequence. Reality and surface grammar define the set, as well as the use or function of a given label in a given combinatory potential. The description of sets makes evident the available patterns of surface grammar to generate messages when the members of any given set are selected in speech, as well as describing what combinations the Spanish language permits.

The decision as to what constitutes the primary distinguishing characteristic is determined by the nature of reality. The dominant feature is not necessarily a scientific description, and it may include some cultural features.

Six major sets are defined by Thornton Kiraithe (1971), although the study was based on an overview of all of the forms marked 'verb' in Spanish. Because of the limits of time, space, and manageability, only three major sets are dealt with here, and then only very superficially.

The sets 'be' and 'become' are so labeled because they express the ideas of 'to be, to get, to grow, to turn, to become', with copula. The very large number of these symbols is of primary importance; there are approximately 600 members of the set 'be' and approximately 1,500 members of the set 'become'. The existence of these sets is a feature of Spanish linguistic organization which has heretofore gone almost entirely unnoticed and has not been exploited in analyses of the language.

Philosophically, in English, 'be' is a sentence-forming element. As a copula, it represents an equal sign--connective words are used to make the relationship between 'John--tall', 'he--sick', 'he--acting' and so forth. The semantic information is carried by the predicate adjective or the gerund form. The most commonly used words to fulfill this same function in Spanish are <u>ser</u>, <u>estar</u>, <u>haber</u>, and <u>tener</u>, in their respective combinatory potentials. However, approximately 600 other labels in Spanish give the same information: 'be' + a noun of occupation (<u>hornear</u> 'to be a baker'); 'be' + an adjective describing an attribute of the subject (<u>encopetarse</u> 'to be conceited'); 'be' + a locative phrase (<u>distar</u> 'to be far'); or 'be' + an adjective phrase (<u>enlutarse</u> 'to be dressed in mourning'). Additionally, the other labels included in this set cover the whole spectrum of other existing sets in the Spanish verb system, and may be cross-referenced with any or all other sets.

An example of only one subset is given here: 'be' + noun. The symbols which comprise this subset express such ideas as adonizar 'to be a dandy' and brujear 'to be a witch'. Human subjects are required, and there are no objects; thus the verbs are labeled intransitive. Each of the labels listed may be transformed by the use of ser, i.e. abogadear 'to be a poor lawyer, to be a shyster' may also be expressed by ser un abogado malo (o engañoso). Interestingly enough, many of these labels express somewhat pejorative ideas or have otherwise unpleasant connotations; when 'to be a lawyer' is meant in approbation, the choice is always ser abogado.

In addition, all of the members of this subset may be found in progressive constructions, in which case the auxiliary estar is required as in any progressive form. As a final note, only eight of the labels in this subset do not have an infinitive in -ear, which has been characterized by Ramsey (1956:646) as having a frequentative value, that is, in this specific case, an extra nuance of 'always'.

Some of the other members of this subset are listed. Obviously, these labels are only members of this subset when the conditions stated above are met.

> adonizar 'to be a dandy'
> brujear 'to be a witch'
> cobardear 'to be a coward'
> jaquear 'to be a braggart'
> ladronear 'to be a thief'
> majear 'to be a bully'
> picardear 'to be a knave or rascal'
> piratear 'to be a pirate'

Several terms which translate the idea of 'get, grow, turn, or become' have been well explained in various treatments of Spanish grammar. These verbs, which are cover words for the set 'become', are hacerse, llegar a ser, ponerse, resultar(se), tornar(se), quedarse, volverse, and in philosophy, devenir. What has not been thoroughly explored is the fact that nearly 1,500 Spanish symbols have as their referents a specific change in status which is reflected by the translation 'get, grow, turn, or become' without recourse to any function word; that is, the verb label itself, under the conditions specific to each subset, signifies the idea of change + some attribute of the subject.

Set 'become' is divided into seven major subsets, which in turn could be further subdivided; however, they are not, since this preliminary division serves to identify the major areas of concern.

Each subset reflects some sort of change: cognitive (apasionarse 'to become impassioned'); changes in color, form, or chemical makeup in inanimate nonsentient entities (acornar 'to become horn shaped or horny'); physiological changes in animate entities (people or animals) (debilitarse 'to become weak'); changes of position or location (yuxtaponerse 'to become juxtaposed'); changes in social status or activities (asociarse 'to become associated'); changes in the weather (anublarse 'to become cloudy'); and changes that may take any subject capable of being changed in the way mentioned (popularizarse 'to become popularized').

With very few exceptions, the process of becoming reflects an involuntary action; therefore, it is not possible to restate these symbols in terms of hacerse, which indicates some effort on the part of the subject, or llegar a ser, which describes normal procedures.

Almost all of the members of this set may be used in different combinatory potentials, with a resulting change in both surface grammar and meaning. For example, when there is a different subject and object, so that the change is effected upon another entity, the verb becomes transitive: Él se adereza 'he gets ready', but Juan adereza los documentos 'John gets the documents ready'.

The subset which deals with changes on the cognitive level (350 members) is the largest of the subsets. Unless it is specifically indicated that the same type of change may take place in an animal, all of the members of this subset require human subjects. Reflexive constructions are required to generate the meaning given; however, this is a nonsystemic reflexive usage, and seems to indicate more than anything else the case of involvement, although at times an external force may be exerting some influence: Se amargó después de que murió su esposa 'he became bitter after his wife died'.

For this subset, possible reformulations are with ponerse, quedarse, and volverse. The members of the subset are too numerous to be presented at this time; therefore, only a few examples are given.

    aquietarse 'to become calm'
    capacitarse 'to become enabled, become qualified'
    depravarse 'to become depraved'
    emborricarse, aborricarse 'to get all confused'
    ennoblecerse 'to become ennobled'
    habituarse 'to become habituated, become more accustomed'
    intranquilizarse 'to become disquieted'
    nausearse 'to become disgusted'
    realizarse 'to become fulfilled'

Another set is relatively small, having approximately 100 members, but is of great interest because it expresses the ideas 'to do again', 'to do repeatedly', or 'to do at a certain time'. No existence of this set has been previously noted. It consists of symbols which carry no live morpheme to mark the ideas of 'again', 'repeatedly', or 'at a certain time', yet each member of the set conveys one of those ideas, e.g.:

'again': binar 'to plow again, to plow a second time'
'repeatedly': campanear 'to ring the bells repeatedly'
'at a certain time': agostar 'to plow to get rid of August weeds', 'to spend August', 'to graze on stubbles in the dry season'

The Spanish morpheme re- regularly appears as a prefix with the meaning 'again', as in rehacer 'to do or make again', or as a prefix which acts as an intensifier (rebueno). In many other verbs, the re- is a dead morpheme because it no longer functions with those meanings (e.g. retener 'to retain', in which re- only marks the difference between mantener, sostener, obtener, tener, etc.). There are approximately 250 verbs marked with re- in which the morpheme continues to function with the meaning 'again' and thus to provide a way to express otra vez within the verb label itself. Such verbs are not listed as members of this set because they belong to a well-recognized morphological pattern which has lexical status.

In three cases, however, there are verbs which use the prefix re- to provide a more specialized meaning: rediezmar 'to tithe a second time' and retacar 'to hit (the ball) a second time (billiards)' provide a slightly more specific meaning. Rebinar 'to earth up (plow) for the third time' derives the idea of 'third time' from a combination of two morphemes: re- 'again' and bi- 'two'.

Three subsets may be defined: (A) the action occurs at a point in time or during an interval of time, (B) the number of times the action is done is specified, and (C) continual, repetitive performance of the same activity. For example, in subset (B), symbols describe the doing of an action for the first, second, or third time; or describe some interval of time at which a specific action is performed. All subjects are animate; the objects come from a variety of sets which must depend upon the logic required by the action described by the verb label. It is noteworthy that only twelve of the terms within this subset do not apply to agriculture or a related action of processing.

Conclusion. The underlying logic which makes it possible to repeat patterns throughout the language is based on what is possible in reality. Men are capable of planting and tending what is planted. But they are not capable of wilting (in the same manner as do plants), or of dropping off the vine. Since the culture recognizes these facts, it accounts for them not only with different terminology, but also with different structural possibilities.

The different structural possibilities become regularized within the system, because without this kind of regularity, communication would be less organized and subsequently it would be more difficult to encode and decode messages.

The importance of the existence of sets of referents of Spanish verbs, then, can be said to lie in the fact that the native speaker organizes his reality in linguistic structures by combining these sets with entities to generate meaningful messages. When Chomsky, Hadlich, and others discuss the theory of competence and the relevance of distinctive features to such a theory, they are in essence talking about the native's selection process which organizes linguistic sets. It is, however, important to understand the precoding decision-making which accounts for this system (distinctive features must come before the encoding process), and not to analyze only on the encoded level.

It is obvious that no speaker of Spanish knows or uses all members of all sets, but it is equally obvious that most speakers (within their own personal limitations) can identify most members of all sets and by analogy, use them properly if they have made the preliminary identification at the precoding level.

The information obtained for this study included examination of every verb label in the Spanish system, and is therefore not based merely on a sampling. However, for presentation purposes, only a selected sampling can be treated. For example, the actual size of the sets could only be determined by a total analysis of the verb lexicon. Sampling procedures would not have revealed the approximately 2,100 members of the sets 'be' and 'become', and would not have revealed the systemwide patterns of usage. Or, whether an event was transitive or intransitive was not a criterion in the establishment of major sets and subsets. However, almost invariably (exceptions such as one questionable label in a subset of 100), when a set was established on the basis of a particularly distinguishing feature as well as the ability of its members to combine with a given set of subjects, then all members of the set or subset would be either transitive or intransitive. Therefore, transitive versus intransitive would appear to be a feature of the sets of referents of Spanish verbs.

In short, investigation of the sets of referents of Spanish verb labels opens the possibility of extracting greater information about structural possibilities within the language in what may well be a more economic method than has been previously undertaken.

REFERENCES

Bergen, John. 1971. Set theory applied to Spanish entity labels. Unpublished doctoral dissertation, University of California, Los Angeles.

Bull, William E. 1965. Spanish for teachers; Applied linguistics. New York, Ronald Press Company.

_____. 1968. Time, tense, and the verb. Berkeley and Los Angeles, University of California Press.

Chafe, Wallace L. 1970. Meaning and the structure of language. Chicago, University of Chicago Press.

Chase, Stuart. 1938. The tyranny of words. New York, Harcourt, Brace and World, Inc.

Chomsky, Noam. 1965. Aspects of the theory of syntax. Cambridge, MIT Press.

_____. 1968a. Language and mind. New York, Harcourt, Brace and World, Inc.

_____. 1968b. Syntactic structures. (Janua linguarum, 4.) The Hague, Mouton.

Diccionario de la Real Academia de España. 1968. Madrid, Gredos.

Fillmore, Charles J. 1968. Lexical entries for verbs. Foundations of Language 4.373-393.

Greenberg, Joseph H., ed. 1966. Universals of language. Cambridge, MIT Press.

Hadlich, Roger L. 1971. A transformational grammar of Spanish. Englewood Cliffs, Prentice-Hall, Inc.

Harris, Zelig. 1966. Structural linguistics. Chicago, University of Chicago Press.

Joos, Martin. 1968. The English verb: Form and meaning. Madison, University of Wisconsin Press.

Katz, Jerrold J. and Jerry A. Fodor. 1964. The structure of a semantic theory. In: The structure of language. Ed. by Katz and Fodor. Englewood Cliffs, Prentice-Hall, Inc.

_____ and Paul M. Postal. 1964. An integrated theory of linguistic description. Cambridge, MIT Press.

Lapesa, Rafael. 1959. Historia de la lengua española. Madrid, Escelicer, S.A.

Mauss, Marcel. 1964. On language and primitive forms of class. In: Language in culture and society. Ed. by Dell Hymes. New York, Harper and Row.

McCawley, James E. 1968. The role of semantics in a grammar. In: Universals of linguistic theory. Ed. by Emmon Bach and Robert T. Harms. New York, Holt, Rinehart and Winston, Inc.

Molina, Hubert. 1970. A model of a pedagogical grammar. Unpublished dissertation, University of California, Los Angeles.

Moliner, María. 1966. Diccionario de uso del español. Madrid, Gredos.

Ogden, C. K. and I. A. Richards. 1923. The meaning of meaning. New York, Harcourt, Brace and World, Inc.

Sánchez Sadek, Carmen and Hildebrando Villarreal. 1972. Set theory applied to event labels. Working paper. University of California, Los Angeles.

Stockwell, Robert P., J. Donald Bowen, and John W. Martin. 1965. The grammatical structures of English and Spanish. Chicago, University of Chicago Press.

Thornton (Kiraithe), Jacqueline M. 1971. A semantic classification, by sets, of the referents of selected Spanish verbs and their structural implications. Unpublished dissertation, University of California, Los Angeles.

Weinreich, Uriel. 1968. Explorations in semantic theory. In: Current trends in linguistics, III. Ed. by Thomas A. Sebeok. The Hague, Mouton.

Whorf, Benjamin Lee. 1969. Language, thought, and reality. Ed. by John B. Carroll. Cambridge, MIT Press.

GRAMMAR:
FROM DESCRIPTION TO EXPLANATION

CARMEN SÁNCHEZ SADEK
University of Southern California

HILDEBRANDO VILLARREAL
University of California at Los Angeles

Stockwell, Bowen, and Martin in their introductory chapter to The Grammatical Structures of English and Spanish indicate that the word 'grammar' has been used to designate a wide variety of distinct kinds of descriptive studies. As a descriptive study a grammar is, according to these authors, a treatise in which the output, verbal or written, of the speakers of a language is classified and described. In other words a grammar is a collection of statements which indicate how samples of speech or writing already spoken or written have been analyzed.

Stockwell, Bowen, and Martin (1965:2-16) have also identified six different types of descriptive grammars. These are: (1) usage grammar; (2) signals grammar; (3) slot-and-substitution grammar; (4) finite-state grammar; (5) phrase structure grammar; and (6) transformational grammar.[1]

The statements which appear in a grammar are referred to as grammar rules. For example, in Spanish the rule 'Adjectives agree in gender with the noun they modify' is a grammar rule which describes a characteristic of certain Spanish forms, namely, when an adjective has two forms bueno/buena the terminal phoneme in the adjective matches the terminal phoneme in the noun libro bueno/casa buena (Bull 1965:105-6). The rule 'A noun is the name of a person, place, or thing' is a grammar rule which states the criteria to be used to classify certain language forms. Phrase structure rules and transformational rules also serve to analyze language forms found in samples of speech or writing already spoken or written (Hadlich 1971:5-6).

Rules postulated on the basis of an analysis of utterances already spoken or written serve to describe linguistic forms and their arrangements with primary stress on the surface features of such forms. A grammarian who abides by the definition of a descriptive grammar studies linguistic output with the purpose of identifying 'interrelated principles which account for the observed data' (Goldin 1968:2). Such a grammarian, however, will not study linguistic output with the purpose of identifying the principles which explain the performance of speakers actually communicating real messages.

It is our contention that a grammar which explains the performance of speakers actually communicating real messages may be a more useful tool for language analysis. In this article we will try to present and illustrate this view and its implications for language study and research.

In 1948 Hockett, in a review of 'A Note on Structure' advocated turning away from the narrow view of the linguistic phenomena studied in descriptive grammars:

The purpose is not simply to account for all the utterances which comprise (one's) corpus at a given time; a simple alphabetical list would do that. Rather, the analysis of the linguistic scientist is to be of such a nature that the linguist can account also for utterances which are not in his corpus at a given time. That is, as a result of his examination, he must be able to predict what other utterances the speakers of the language might produce, and ideally, the circumstances under which those other utterances might be produced (Hockett 1948:269).

More recently, John B. Carroll has also emphasized the need for a redefinition of the linguistic phenomena and for an evaluation of the types of rules resulting from formal analysis of languages. He considers language systems as a means for thinking and talking about objective and possible reality. He thinks that language analysis should deal with units of expression directly related to the world of experience, be it real, potential or imaginary, and that one set of linguistic rules should deal with the kinds of experiences which are encoded by language labels. Carroll also indicates that in language analysis it is not usually necessary to specify the context, verbal or nonverbal, of linguistic expressions. As a result, he appears to believe that this type of language analysis gives the impression that the language system can operate in a kind of situationless vacuum in which there are neither stimuli nor responses. According to Carroll one is tempted to overlook the problem of what kinds of nonlinguistic situations prompt sentences. He also believes that the main point of contact between the linguistic system and reality comes to be thought of as being in the 'semantic component'. More precisely, the analysis of the contact between the linguistic system and reality is relegated to a 'semantic component' that gets shoved aside in favor of what Carroll defines as the seemingly more exciting and tractable problems of syntax (Carroll 1970:16).

Goldin (1968:3) has made an analogy between the grammarian and the computer expert, but with one important difference. The computer expert, confronted with a computer in operation, can examine the input and output, and can discover the program according to which the computer is presently operating, that is, the particular instructions under which the machine is functioning. The grammarian, on the other hand, when confronted with speakers, can observe their output but, unlike the computer expert, he can only make assumptions about the individual grammar, that is, the instructions under which the speaker is operating. In the analogy of the computer, meaning corresponds roughly to input, and form to output. The computer program relates input to output and the grammar of the language relates meaning to form. Some transformationalists state that they are not yet able to assert everything they might like to say about meaning. They have postulated a level intermediate between meaning and form which they call, following Chomsky, 'deep structure' and the principles relating deep structure to surface structure are transformational rules.

Some transformationalists, then, appear to accept the idea that semantics encompasses much more than can be described by deep structure and hope that as more and more is learned about semantics and its relation to syntax, there will be less and less need for an intermediate level of deep structure. [2] However, and this may be the major limitation of transformational grammar in our opinion, for the time being they make the assumption 'that deep structure provides all the information relevant to the semantic interpretation of the sentence' (Goldin 1968:3). Lakoff (1968:4) has suggested several conditions for defining deep structure. [3]

Taken together, the assumptions made by the transformationalists, if we understand Goldin, have not permitted them, as Hockett stated, 'to predict what other utterances the speakers of the language might produce and the circumstances under which those other utterances might be produced.'

William E. Bull (1968b:225) has indicated that:

For the descriptive linguist speech is the reality being analyzed. Classes or sets defined in descriptive analyses are primarily determined by the number of contrastive features in the formal structure of the speech system. The criteria for classification may be the combinatory potential of the feature (he requires the form talks, not talk in the indicative) or meaning (talked is semantically different from talks). However, when one part of the contrasting forms (in this case the stem talk) may be replaced by other items (walk, contrast, rake, etc. . . . without systemic consequences, the communication function of the members of this set is treated as irrelevant to the purpose of formal descriptive linguistics. In other words, a relationship between the speech system and reality is established only when it is necessary to account for some feature of the system, and since the number and kinds of these features are determined largely by historical accident, a linguistic description of the system provides very little information about how speech is used to organize objective reality. No formal grammar, in short, can explain why a perfectly grammatical sentence (Our fence talks Spanish) can be utter nonsense in one universe of discourse (the back yard) and completely meaningful in another (a den of thieves).

According to Bull (1968b: 213-228) none of the grammars presented by Stockwell, Bowen, and Martin includes rules which permit the generation of novel sentences since none of them deals with the two systems which must be mastered in order to communicate. [4] One system is speech and the other is what speech talks about, reality. The features of both systems, speech and reality, are divided into sets whose interactions must be understood before communication is possible. No novel sentences can be generated or understood unless both the speaker and the hearer recognize the sets to which all features of both systems belong.

Linguists are beginning to recognize the need to deal with meaning in their descriptions of language. Wallace E. Chafe (1967:57) has indicated that the theories of language postulated by Fodor and Katz in 1964 and by Chomsky in 1965 arose 'from a preoccupation with the symbol, rather than with that which is symbolized' and as a result such theories distorted 'the real relationship between the two', that is, the symbol and the referent of the symbol. Chafe (1967:57-8) regards language

. . . as a particular case of the set of abilities which allow animals to communicate, to transfer information from one individual to another . . . Any particular item of information which is communicated from one organism to another is called a message and messages originate in

experience. Experience is the entire realm of internal states
and processes, cognitions and emotions, from which messages
can be assembled.

According to Chafe communication begins with a message in the universe of experience which, for some reason, is to be communicated.
The communication system provides a way for this message to be
symbolized within the universe of sound or of another medium (often
this process has been thought to be a kind of 'encoding'). The symbol
next passes to some other individual by whom it is 'decoded' into a
facsimile, reasonable or otherwise, of the original message. Chafe
asserts that 'encoding' and 'decoding' are essentially mirror images
and, consequently, the study of a communication system can be con-
centrated on either process.

Once Chafe has established this model of coding, which is communication based on experience, he appears to run into trouble. He
asserts that experience has its seat almost entirely within the human
brain and that its correlation with externally observable human behavior is minimal and largely unenlightening. He asks: 'Can we
then make experimental observations which have objective validity,
or is introspection, our chief instrument for such observations, a
wholly subjective and whimsical technique?' (Chafe 1967:63). He
recommends introspection as the way to explore experience and as
the way to test the validity of our conclusions about experience.

The model of communication proposed by Bull is similar to that
of Chafe. However, the differences between the two models must be
understood to grasp the power of Bull's model. Bull's model includes three basic processes: precoding, encoding, and decoding.
Briefly outlined, the model goes like this: A speaker wants to say
something about a certain reality, let's say a group of persons. He
observes this reality and its organization. Specifically he observes
certain features which his culture has taught him are important in
talking about this reality. For example, if the speaker is a Spaniard,
he will notice features such as (a) the group is made up of animate
entities, persons, to be precise; (b) the group is made up of persons
of a certain age, let's assume 50 years or older; (c) a certain sex,
all are men; (d) a certain social rank, all are professionals, etc.
The speaker will also pay attention to the features in the social
situation in which he finds himself which his culture considers important in sending messages. For example, the speaker will notice
(a) the subject of discourse which has been maintained up to the time
he is ready to communicate his message. In other words, has any
mention been made of the group of persons he is going to talk about
or is he talking about this group of people for the first time in the
conversation?; (b) the visual focus of his listeners, that is, are the

listeners focusing their eyes on the subject of discourse he is going to talk about or must the speaker in his message say something to focus his listeners' attention on the subject of discourse?; (c) the attitude of the listeners. For example, what will the listeners' reaction be to the subject of discourse?

Finally, the speaker will decide what he wants to say about these persons. Let's say he wants to communicate something about where they are located. Certain features concerning the location of the entities must be considered by the speaker: (a) the distance of the entities from the speaker: close, near, or far; (b) the type of space in which the entities are located: shaped or enclosed space; (c) the role of the entities within the space: spectators or performers. The speaker will also determine what information he needs to emphasize in the message. The message might be that: 'some men are in a certain place' or that: 'some men are in a certain place'. For English speakers intonation will mark this emphasis and for Spanish speakers the position of the phrase within the utterance will accomplish the same goal.

Bull names this phase of the communication process 'precoding'. In precoding the speaker perceives and pays attention to certain critical features both in the reality he is going to talk about and in the social situation which are relevant for sending messages he wishes to communicate. In the example we have used so far we have assumed that the critical features the speaker must perceive and react to are: a group of entities, animate, persons, all males 50 years or older, well dressed professionals, no prior mention in the conversation about the entities and no shared knowledge about the entities, no unfavorable reaction expected from the listener, the location of the entities is far away from both the speaker and the listener. The essence of the message is 'some people (men) are at a certain location'. When the speaker has made all of the above observations he then refers to the language system to determine how this system allows him to 'encode' the message he wants to communicate. The language system or structure may offer different ways to encode this message. Once a way of sending the message is chosen, then the system requires certain arbitrary conventions. To encode the message outlined above the speaker may say:

Allí hay unos señores.
'Some men are there.'

or

Allí acaban de llegar unos señores.
'Some men have just arrived there.'

Both messages convey the same general idea. The precoding phase signaled the choice of señores but not hombres; unos but not los; unos señores in final position in the utterance but not initial or medial. The language system requires n after acaba to match señores, and unos señores after hay but not before.

When the message encoded by the speaker reaches the listener, it is decoded, that is, the listener forms a mental image of the reality the speaker is talking about. In the particular example illustrated here the listener will, upon hearing allí hay unos señores, decode that a new subject of discourse has been introduced and that he must focus his attention on this subject of discourse. The speaker said unos and this will cue the listener to search for a group of persons matching the features encoded by the word señores; people of a certain age, sex, social rank, professional affiliation, and so forth; the listener will look for entities 'far' from himself and the speaker, allí; and the listener will understand that the meaning of the message is 'people there'.

In Bull's model successful communication is defined in terms of the speaker's ability to encode the message in such a way that the listener decodes the message intended by the speaker. This ability is based on the speaker's perception of the reality he wants to talk about and its organization, and also on the speaker's knowledge about how this reality accounts for the existence and the function of the forms of his language.

The similarities and differences between Bull's and Chafe's models can now be outlined. Both postulate models which include encoding, communication through language, and decoding. Both are concerned with the relationship between symbol (language) and what is symbolized, 'experience' for Chafe and 'reality' for Bull. The power of Bull's model stems from this postulation of reality as the point of departure in message sending and from his definition of precoding as the mental process in which the relevant features of this reality are abstracted and become the basis for the choice of language forms.

Bull's model of communication is significant in three respects. First, it permits the discovery of the features in reality which signal the choice of forms in the specific language. Reality includes specific objects or entities, actions, events, interactions (stimulus response situations), social context, verbal context, attitudes of the speakers and listeners, etc. The descriptions of those features in reality which signal the choice of language forms will result in the postulation of concepts which are relevant to understanding the role of language in actual communication. Thus in:

Aquí hay unos señores 'Some men are here'
Aquí están los señores 'The men are here'

the verbal context in which the speaker is going to communicate his message signals the choice of unos or los. If the speaker is going to talk about a subject of discourse not previously mentioned in the conversation or not previously observed by his listeners, and if the speaker and listener share no common knowledge about this subject of discourse, then the speaker uses unos. The description provided can be summarized by the concept 'initiation of common focus' (Bull 1965:216). If the speaker is going to talk about a subject of discourse previously mentioned in the conversation or, if not previously mentioned, the listener has his attention focused on the referent of the subject of discourse to be introduced or, if both listener and speaker share common knowledge about the subject of discourse then the speaker uses los. This can be summarized by the concept 'maintenance of common focus' (Bull 1965:216). When the speaker has chosen, depending on the features of the verbal context, the forms he needs to communicate his message, then the system demands the arbitrary cooccurrence of hay with unos and están with los.

Second, Bull's model permits a redefinition of the subject matter of grammar or linguistics. The description of language per se can now become the description of the function of language in message sending. Rules and generalizations based exclusively on the formal combinatory potential of contrastive features can now be extended to include how the semantic potential of the contrastive features are directly related to the ordinary business of message sending. The subject matter of linguistics in this model includes both language and reality encompassing nonlinguistic fields such as physics, psychology, and sociology. From physics the linguist borrows concepts related to the nature of events (aspect: initiative, imperfective, and terminative) to explain the uses of the subjunctive in Spanish. From sociology the linguist borrows concepts of group structure (rank, relation, etc.) to explain the uses of tú and usted.

Finally, Bull's model of communication permits a redefinition of the concepts of language universals and competence. Since reality, as defined in its broadest terms, is the point of departure in the analysis of language, contrastive studies of different languages have, consequently, the same point of departure, the same reality. If a certain feature in this reality is important for choosing language forms in all languages contrasted, then the description of that feature and the concepts postulated from such a description become a language universal. As an illustration, limiting ourselves to English and Spanish, the category to which an individual belongs is an important feature which must be taken into consideration in sending messages. In Spanish, the idea of category is expressed by a noun in the singular without modification: José es profesor 'Joe is a professor'. José is or equals member of the category 'professor'. In other words, <u>profesor</u> labels the category to which <u>José</u> belongs. English, however, expresses the same idea by indicating that <u>José</u> is one of the members of the category 'professor' and, as a result, marks the noun with a number determiner: <u>Joe is a professor</u>. A concept such as category becomes a universal when, through comparative studies, it is found to be important for the choice of language forms and is marked in languages through surface features, lexicon, or suprasegmental features. Compare:

José es payaso.	(member of a category)
2 3 1	
'Joe is a clown.'	(member of a category)
José es un payaso.	(acting as a clown)
3 3 1	
'Joe is a clown.'	(acting as a clown)

Bull has shown that in talking about events most of the major languages of the world express concepts such as 'prime axis of orientation' (moment of speaking), 'retrospective axis of orientation' (point in the past), 'anticipated axis of orientation' (point anticipated from the moment of speaking), and 'retrospective anticipated axis of orientation' (point anticipated at time of recollection). He has also shown that languages express order relationships to these axes, anterior, posterior, and simultaneous, as well as aspects of events (Bull 1968a: 20-24). All of these concepts are expressed at the level of surface features in English and Spanish by the markers of tenses or are marked by the lexicon. Compare:

Lo habrá hecho mañana a la una 'He will have done it by one
    o'clock tomorrow'
Lo hará mañana antes de la una 'He will do it before one
    o'clock tomorrow'

Both of these sentences convey the same idea: at an anticipated point in the future an event will be terminated. In the first sentence these ideas are conveyed by the verb forms. In the second sentence the verb form marks only anticipation. The adverb serves to mark, lexically, the termination of the event.

The concept of language competence can now be redefined in light of the concept of language universals, which are learned by all speakers of a language. This knowledge of universals, although intuitive in nature, is readily manifested by speakers in the choice of language forms. As indicated in the previous example, language systems offer several ways of expressing the same concepts. Competence, then, can be defined in terms of the number of alternatives which are available in the speaker's system to express particular concepts. Speakers vary in terms of the number of ways which they command to express a particular concept. For some speakers the choice habrá hecho is not available in their repertoire of forms to indicate an event terminated at an anticipated point. For other speakers both possibilities are available, habrá hecho and hará antes. The second speaker can be said to approximate in his performance the 'potential' of the system to a greater degree than the first speaker.

Several implications of this definition of competence--or better, potential--should now be pointed out. Potential is a property of the language, that is, it refers to the possible ways of expressing certain concepts. This feature of the system is, however, independent of the users of the system. In other words, all alternatives are available to every speaker. No single individual, nonetheless, commands the total number of choices the language system offers. No one person can exploit all of the possibilities. Some alternatives are used only by highly sophisticated writers.

Potential, as defined here, has been divorced from human performance. It does not refer to an attribute of the speaker, the competence of the speaker, but rather, to an attribute of the language system.

So far we have indicated that reality defined in its broadest terms cues the choice of forms in communicating a message. It was also shown that the language system offers alternate ways of expressing the same message, that is, different ways of encoding. Now, a brief look around our environment will indicate that the possible 'realities' we can talk about are infinite and, consequently, the various ways of expressing these realities is very large. The human brain has devised a way to cope with this array of realities and forms. Bull's model of communication defines this coping device as 'set theory'.

The basic notions of set theory can be understood if, as noted before, attention is paid to the complexity of the world about which messages are communicated. Bull (1965:131) states:

When one stops to consider the fact that the number of symbols in Spanish is extremely large (several hundred thousand) and that the number of different possible combinations is literally astronomical, it immediately becomes apparent that no Spaniard could possibly manage either the symbols or their combinations if each had to be dealt with as a unique item. To deal with such potential complexity, and especially at the speed of speech, each symbol must belong to some category, the number of categories must be relatively small, and combinations must be treated primarily as combinations of categories rather than as individual items.

The categories Bull is referring to are of two kinds: sets and systems. Systems are categories 'composed of items which are alike and different in relation to the same principle' (Bull 1965:132). For instance, the adjectives poco, mucho, and todo represent a system. All three adjectives deal with amount and, at the same time, the three adjectives differ from each other in terms of the same principle: amount.

Sets are categories 'composed of items which are alike and different in relation to totally unrelated principles' (Bull 1965:132). For example, alto, largo, and mucho are alike, first, because they are adjectives and, second, because they end in the same syntactic differentiator o. However, as symbols they are radically different. Largo deals with length, alto with height, and mucho with amount. These words are then members of a set.

All speakers of a language recognize and understand the sets and systems which the language marks. The culture uses, in defining sets and systems, criteria and features which can be readily observed and learned at a very early age by all speakers of the language. Usually these criteria and cues are associated with some cultural universal.

Sets or systems may be established, according to Bull (1965:132), in terms of three factors:

(1) What exists in objective reality: animals, plants, minerals, the three dimensions of space, things that can be counted, etc.,
(2) How the culture organizes reality: the metric system, familial relationships, calendar, etc.
(3) Purely linguistic phenomena: syntactic differentiators, parts of speech, classes of verbs, types of affixes, etc.

All items that belong to a set share common features. For example. Norwegian, tea cup, and pig are three items that belong to the same set. In reality the referents of these three words stand for entities that can be counted. In other words, the referents of these three words share the feature countable entities. These three items belong to the set count entities. This set has been established according to the first factor mentioned above, objective reality.

Sets can be divided into subsets. The members of the set count entities can be subdivided into animate (Norwegian, pig) and inanimate (tea cup). The animate set can be subdivided into persons and animals. Members of a given set are semantically similar, that is, they share more features in common than members of different subsets but within the same set. Thus, 'horse' shares more features in common with 'pig' (animal, animate, count entity) than with 'Norwegian' (person, animate, count entity) although all the items mentioned belong to the same set (animate, count entities) (Bergen 1971:19).

The cues which define sets and systems can be identified at different levels of generalization. For example, all trees belong to a grand set, members of which can be identified as having green leaves, dark trunks, and branches, and having the potential of growing to be large objects five feet or more in height. Most people use these cues in identifying the members of the set trees. Some people, however, are able to react to cues such as the shape and color of the leaves, the type of flower, if any, and thus are able to identify avocado, apple, orange, plum, pine trees, etc.

It was indicated above that all speakers of a language recognize and understand the sets and systems which the language marks. From the above explanation of the different levels of generalization which can be used to define sets and subsets, it is clear that all speakers intuitively know the grand sets marked by the language. All speakers distinguish between members of the set trees and members of the set shrubs. Only some speakers can make more refined distinctions within these two grand sets.

Linguistically, forms belonging to the same set share the same combinatory potential and forms of different sets have different combinatory potentials. In other words, all the forms of a set can be combined with forms of another set without changing the meaning which results from this combination. For example, members of the set containers combine with members of the set liquids with the resulting meaning 'container for liquid' or 'liquid in container'.

Set: Container		Set: Liquids
botella	de	agua
lata		leche
vaso		vino
pomo		aceite

Changing any of the members in the sets in the above combinations with a member from another set results in a change in meaning. For example, the set container with the set materials generates the meaning 'container made of . . .'

Set: Container		Set: Materials
botella	de	vidrio
lata		plástico
vaso		aluminio
pomo		cartón

We can say that 'the subset membership of the forms is defined linguistically by their combinatory potential' (Bergen 1971:19). What this means in practice is that if one form of a set or subset can occupy a given syntactic or morphological slot, then all forms belonging to that same true set or subset may likewise be put in that slot. Of course, forms ultimately exhibit certain combinatory potentials peculiar to each of them alone. The term combinatory potential, as used in the preceding discussion, refers to relationships between sets or subsets, not between individual forms of the sets.

The significance of set theory has been recognized by grammarians. The basis for classification in previous formulations of this theory was the linguistic combinatory potentials of the forms belonging to a set. Transformational linguists recognize that <u>sing</u> and <u>run</u> are verbs of different subsets (Bergen 1971:1-16).

He's running the car.   The car is running.
He's singing a hymn.   *A hymn is singing.

The transformationalists did not look at the events that <u>run</u> and <u>sing</u> stand for. Such an analysis would have resulted in a description of the common features shared by these events (capable of being performed by animate entities, humans in particular) as well as a description of their differences (<u>running</u> stands for an event involving linear movement which can be performed by a mechanical device under the control of the referent for subject of the sentence, 'he runs the car'; <u>singing</u> stands for an event involving vocalization of melodies and can only be performed by a doer or by a musical instrument). This type of analysis would have identified in reality the sets to which the two events belong. As members of different sets their combinatory potentials, at the level of language, are consequently different.

Bull's model of communication, including as it does precoding, encoding, decoding, and set theory, could well serve to bring about a redefinition of the linguistic phenomena under consideration in formal language analysis. Rules and concepts postulated on the basis of the analysis of linguistic and nonlinguistic phenomena will be useful for understanding language as it functions in communication. Such concepts and rules will, as Hockett advocates (1948:269), enable us 'to predict what other utterances the speakers of the language might produce and the circumstances under which those utterances might be produced'.

A grammar in which these rules and concepts are presented will no longer be a descriptive study but rather an explanatory study, that is, a treatise in which the causes of the phenomena observed in a particular field of study are given.

NOTES

1. Stockwell, Bowen, and Martin give the following definitions of the different types of grammars: (1) usage grammar is a set of rules to discriminate between educated usage and all other varieties of usage; (2) signals grammar is a classification of the signals which differentiate one sentence from another; (3) slot and substitution grammar is a finite number of sentence patterns, each pattern containing one or more slots within which a corresponding class of lexical units may replace one another; (4) finite-state grammar is a description of the probability relationships between lexical units in sequence; (5) immediate constituent analysis or phrase structure grammar is a description of the degree of closeness or clustering of lexical units in sequence; and (6) transformational grammar is a set of phrase structure rules for the derivation of simple active declarative sentences, combined with a set of transformational rules which, applied to the sentences derived by the phrase structure rules, add to, subtract from, or modify the order within them, or combine them in complex ways.

2. Some transformationalists still adhere to the concept of deep structure (Chomsky, Jackendoff, et al.). They assume that the form of language (i. e. syntax) has properties which are independent of semantics. It has been maintained by people working in this framework that syntax and semantics can be studied independently. On the other hand there are transformationalists who believe that deep structure equals semantic structure, perhaps with some well-formedness conditions.

3. The deep structure conditions Lakoff mentions are: (1) Basic grammatical relations (e. g. subject of, object of) are represented in terms of fundamental grammatical categories. (2) The correct generalizations about the selectional restrictions and cooccurrence can be stated at this level. (3) Lexical items are assigned to their appropriate categories at this level. (4) The structures defined at this level are the input to transformational rules.

4. Bull (1968b: 213-228) illustrates his objections to the six types of grammars described by Stockwell, Bowen, and Martin with an analysis of the sentence The two boys were playing in the yard and

the more than twenty possible translations that this sentence has in Spanish.

REFERENCES

Bergen, John. 1971. Set theory applied to Spanish entity labels.
    Unpublished dissertation, University of California, Los Angeles.
Bull, William E. 1965. Spanish for teachers: Applied linguistics.
    New York, Ronald Press.
_____. 1968a. Time, tense, and the verb: A study in theoretical
    and applied linguistics with particular attention to Spanish.
    Berkeley and Los Angeles, University of California Press.
_____. 1968b. We need a communications grammar. Glossa
    2. 213-28.
Carroll, John B. 1970. Towards a third generation psycholinguistics.
    Paper presented at the American Psychological Association Con-
    vention. Miami Beach.
Chafe, Wallace E. 1967. Language as symbolization. Lg. 43.57-91.
Goldin, Mark G. 1968. Spanish case and function. Washington,
    D.C., Georgetown University Press.
Hadlich, Roger L. 1971. A transformational grammar of Spanish.
    Englewood Cliffs, Prentice-Hall.
Hockett, Charles F. 1948. A note on structure. IJAL 14.269-271.
Lakoff, George. 1968. Instrumental adverbs and the concept of deep
    structure. Foundations of Language 4.4-29.
Stockwell, Robert P., J. Donald Bowen, and John W. Martin. 1965.
    The grammatical structures of English and Spanish. Chicago,
    University of Chicago Press.

LEVELING OF PARADIGMS IN CHICANO SPANISH

MARIO SALTARELLI

University of Illinois

0. Introduction. In the last two years, phonological characteristics of Spanish as spoken in the Southwest of the United States and
other regions has been brought to the attention of generative grammar
(Harris 1973a, 1973b, 1974a, 1974b).

Briefly, when compared with Standard Spanish, this language shows
significant leveling in the verb paradigm, which involves the elimination of the o-ue alternation in all first conjugation verbs with the
result that ue appears in all forms regardless of stress: vuelár 'to
fly', vuclámos 'we fly', etc. as well as vuélo 'I fly', vuélan 'they
fly', etc. Another type of leveling occurs in the subjunctive paradigms, where the first person plural of trabajar 'to work' is
trabájenos instead of the Standard trabajémos.

The data at hand provide an excellent example of the interpene-
tration of phonology, morphology, syntax and the lexicon, lending
itself to testing for the theories of 'natural' phonology, 'abstract'
phonology, and the middle ground theory which reconsiders the
possibility of an autonomous morphological component.

From a diachronic perspective, Chicano offers the linguist a
rare opportunity for observing an ongoing linguistic change as a
function of the system acquired in a weakly monitored sociolin-
guistic environment. This allows testing of the predictions about
general linguistic theory made by different analyses within the
present theory of generative phonology. It provides one of the
empirical bases for evaluating the plausibility of an analysis, consistent with accepted universals of linguistic change.

The Chicano Spanish material is a rich illustration of analogical
leveling. I shall distinguish two types of leveling, one affecting
phonological structure only, the other morphological markers.

123

(1) Phonological Leveling
   (a) Elimination of phonetic alternation through rule loss or rule fading.
   (b) Elimination of phonetic contrasts in given environments (neutralization) through rule extension and rule addition.
(2) Morphological Leveling: Elimination of entire subparadigms or parts of them.

The classic German example bunt:bunde provides us with an example of phonological leveling through rule loss in the case of some dialects of northern Switzerland where the final obstruent devoicing rule is lost resulting in bund:bunde. An example of phonological leveling through rule extension is observed in connection with the same German rule extended also to nonparadigmatic words like (aẙek 'away', Standard German weg (cf. Kiparsky 1968a). For morphological leveling I intend the loss of a subparadigm like the future under certain conditions in Spanish, Italian, and French, the loss of the subjunctive in Italian and French, or the partial loss of a subparadigm like the second person plural in many varieties of Spanish.

1. Leveled paradigms in Chicano. The leveling phenomenon in Chicano, well documented since its inception less than a century ago, is still in a state of geographic and lexical diffusion, especially in areas of the United States where the language has emigrant status only. For the purpose of this paper I rely on the data reported in the papers by J. W. Harris, and on informal observations made in Mexican-American communities in the Chicago area.

Present indicative		Present subjunctive	
vuélo	volámos	vuéle	volémos (Standard)
vuélas		vuéles	
vuéla	vuélan	vuéle	vuélen

vuélo	vuelámos	vuéle	vuélenos (Chicano)
vuélas		vuéles	
vuéla	vuélan	vuéle	vuélen

An uncommitted look at the Standard and Chicano paradigms reveals the following differences:

	Standard	Chicano
Diphthongs	alternating	not alternating
Stress (subj.)	alternating	not alternating
First plural (subj.)	-mos	-nos

Note further that the Standard Spanish diphthongs alternate within the verb paradigm and outside, strictly conditioned by stress, and for a subset of the lexicon only. In Chicano the alternation is eliminated within the paradigm of the first conjugation verbs: infinitive vuelár 'to fly', past participle vueládo, gerund vuelándo, preterite vuelé, imperfect vuelába, past subjunctive vuelára. For forms other than those in the verb paradigm the situation is the same as in Standard Spanish: volador 'flyer', etc. This fact clearly points to the relevance of the paradigm as the environment within which the operation of leveling is confined. Another question about the diphthongs that one might want to ask is the leveling to ue rather than to o. A simple and probably correct answer is that the phenomenon is the effect of the 'majority rule' assumed by traditional theories of analogy. The same statistical principle of the relative size of the three verb classes is suggested as the reason for the leveling starting in first conjugation verbs. Another puzzling fact is that leveling occurs only for o-ue alternations but not e-ie alternations. It is not clear why back vowel alternations should be leveled but not front vowel alternations. One can only offer an historical correlation which seems to effect only back vowels: the C. Latin to Spanish development ó wo we. Because of this change there is an asymmetry between the front and back diphthongs. Front diphthongs ie-e are homorganic, back diphthongs ue-o are not. The leveling in the subjunctive is not amenable to the phonological explanation just suggested for diphthongs. Stress leveling occurs in a statistically low frequency paradigm. This is a case which appears to disprove the claim that analogical leveling begins in statistically high frequency contexts. Finally, the change from -mos to -nos, the unconditioned change from m to n in just one morpheme, is a very improbable phenomenon.

2.0 Competing analyses. Given the Standard and the Chicano Spanish material just discussed, more than one analysis is compatible with the present theory of generative phonology. Aside from answering the question of which analysis yields the 'neatest' solution, I take it to be the central business of linguistic theory to ascertain which of the possible proposals is relatively right or wrong, on the basis of the implicit predictions each analysis makes about the general theory of language. The sources of empirical data for testing the validity of the predictions are language evolution, language acquisition, and the descriptive capacity of the grammatical mechanism, among others. My theoretical argumentation will concentrate mainly on the alternation condition and the relatedness condition as criteria for rule plausibility.

Consider the following two analyses which differ in that the first is a basically phonological solution, the second a morphological one. (For the purpose of discussion I shall label the first simply Phonological Analysis, the second simply Morphological Analysis.)

2.1 Phonological analysis.

(a) 'those instances of e̱ and o̱ marked [+diphthongization rule] are diphthongized if (i) they are stressed, and (ii) if o̱ is in the first conjugation verb stem (stressed or unstressed)' (Harris 1974a:19).
(b) shift to 'columnar' stress in the subjunctive.
(c) m̱ becomes ṉ in the first person plural of the present subjunctive.

2.2 Morphological analysis.

(a) first conjugation o̱-ue verbs are restructured as ue verbs.
(b) first person plural present subjunctive is restructured:
  (i) morphologically: trabáje-nos
  (ii) syntactically: trabáje#nos

The phonological analysis is partially morphologized, and the morphological analysis is partially lexicalized. Both analyses account for the differences between Standard and Chicano Spanish, but they differ sharply in the grammatical characterization of the phenomenon. The theory of generative phonology provides no basis for evaluation. Crude simplicity criteria based on notational predicates like disjunctivity, parentheses, elsewhere condition, and the like have failed to reveal any significant generalization about the nature of language and the form of linguistic theory. In an attempt to decide whether the phonological or the morphological analysis is the correct generalization for the innovations in Chicago, I shall look at the predictions implicit in each analysis.

3.0 Consequences of the phonological analysis

3.1 Diphthongs. As regards diphthongization, the phonological analysis implies that Chicano has acquired a new rule of diphthongization, limited to the back vowel o̱ and applying in the morphological/lexical set of first conjugation verbs. Note that stress is no longer the conditioning factor in this environment.

This implies that the representation of verbs like vuelár, cuentár, etc. will have to be given an underlying o̱-stem which never appears on the surface in any form of the paradigm. The claim made by this analysis is that analogical leveling which involves a simplification of surface phonetic distinctions results in a more complex grammar.

Such prediction is counterintuitive and is contradicted by what is commonly known about the evolution of languages and the process of child language learning.

As for rule innovation, the theory claims that a minor rule (a phenomenon of exception) extends its scope under entirely unrelated conditions like first conjugation verbs. But it is an established fact that the tendency for exceptions of this type is to shrink or disappear. No minor rule seems to be on record that tends to extend in such a way.

It is also a generally known fact about child language acquisition and the evolution of adult speech in emigrant languages that there is a tendency to extend general rules at the expense of minor rules. An example of this trend is the regularization of irregular past participles like <u>morido</u> for <u>muerto</u> 'dead', or the English <u>dived</u> for <u>dove</u> (child and adult language), as well as irregular comparatives like <u>gooder</u> for <u>better</u>. The opposite phenomenon is rarely observed.

The phonological analysis appears to make predictions which are empirically untenable.

3.2 Subjunctive. As for the paradigmatic innovation in the subjunctive, the phonological hypothesis does appear to have an historical precedent in the history of Spanish, namely the imperfect indicative and subjunctive shifted to columnar stress from penultimate stress (Harris 1974b). However, the early Spanish shift does not quite correlate with the Chicano stress shift. If the same phenomenon were at stake, one would expect an equivalent shift in the present indicative, but this is not the case nor is there any indication that there is paradigmatic diffusion of columnar stress. As a trend toward a natural phenomenon one would also need an explanation as to why it started in a low frequency paradigm, which runs contrary to the leveling of diphthongs in first conjugation verbs, a high frequency paradigm. There is independent evidence from borrowing that the size of a lexical class and the frequency of a paradigm are linguistically significant factors. Perhaps the consequence which is most damaging to the phonological analysis of the subjunctive innovation in Chicano is that it forces the grammar to accept the phonologically unconditioned shift from <u>m</u> to <u>n</u> as regular sound change, or else it provides no principled explanation for the innovation in the first person plural ending. Both predictions are obviously unsatisfactory. To accept the <u>m</u> to <u>n</u> as regular sound change is tantamount to blinding oneself to significant achievements in modern historical linguistics, and abandoning any hope for a theory of sound change.

4. Consequences of the morphological analysis. The morphological analysis of diphthongization in Chicano can be defined as a 'concrete' solution as opposed to the phonological 'abstract' solution. I shall not claim that a priori a concrete solution is psychologically more plausible than an abstract analysis. There seems to be, however, some evidence that speakers prefer concrete to abstract analysis given the alternative.

4.1. Consider first the grammar which results from the morphological hypothesis of Chicano diphthongs. The grammar of Chicano incorporates no additional rules of diphthongization (with respect to Standard Spanish); rather the stress conditioned diphthongization rule of Standard Spanish has faded in Chicano, in that its scope no longer ranges over first conjugation o-stem verbs. The analogically leveled verbs are restructured in the lexicon as ue-stem verbs. This analysis is consistent with the common observation that minor rules tend to shrink or fade away by a narrowing of their scope of application brought about by analogical leveling in paradigms. There is evidence that leveling of diphthongization in Chicano Spanish has diffused gradually through the class of first conjugation verbs in the last century or so. There is also evidence that the phenomenon is spreading to other conjugations. We found some forms of the -ir verbs like muerió 'he died' and muerír 'to die'. The restructuring analysis is the only device that can characterize the phenomenon through time with minimal disturbance in the system of rules. That paradigmatic leveling is correctly captured by restructuring is supported by the fact that it provides also an explanation for the fading of another minor rule, the raising of o to u in verbs like 'to play' jugar (infinitive) jugando (gerund), juego (present indicative), which in Chicano are leveled to juegar, juegando, juego.

In sum, the morphological-lexical analysis of Chicano diphthongs makes predictions which are consistent with the known facts about linguistic change, and offers the proper mechanism for the on-going lexical diffusion of the phenomenon with resulting fading and eventually possible disappearance of the rule from the grammar. This solution supports the claim that paradigm leveling is reflected in the simplification of grammars and not in their complication.

4.2. The morphological-syntactic solution to the Chicano innovations in the subjunctive claims that the grammatical analysis of the first person plural is restructured in one of two ways: (a) the ending -mos is replaced by -nos by the commonly accepted principle of morphological 'supplition', or (b) the form is syntactically reanalyzed as two words trabáje#nos.

Intuitively, I waver between the morphological and the syntactic solution. What kind of predictions and/or empirical data can be adduced to weaken or strengthen one solution over the other?

The morphological supplition analysis, although planted in tradition, does not really suggest what type of analogical pressure in the paradigm could be responsible for the supplition phenomenon. I believe an inkling of motivation could be attributed to the analogy with the third person plural morpheme -n, but you would have a difficult time answering questions like: why in the subjunctive only? is there any other such case known? why didn't the third person plural morpheme change to -m instead?

The syntactic solution claims that the language has developed a special locution for exhortative imperatives, with the consequence that the subjunctive paradigm no longer has a first plural form. What can be said about this? There is a relatively recent precedent for elimination of morphological distinctions within a paradigm: the loss of second person plural in a large number of Spanish dialects. Thus the morphological leveling receives a certain degree of credibility in Chicano Spanish. There is also a well defined syntactic conditioning factor in which the phenomenon occurs: inclusive exhortations like vámonos. Finally, the surface appearance of the forms lends itself to the analysis of a subjunctive verb form without person and number inflection plus a first person plural pronoun nos.

Both the morphological and the syntactic solution seem to be in compliance with the way languages usually change, to a degree astronomically higher than the phonological solution. A program for choosing between the morphological and the syntactic solution would have to look for psychological evidence that speakers perceive forms like trabájenos as two words or one word.

5. Relatedness condition. The phonological analysis can be subjected to further linguistic-theoretic arguments involving two fundamental conditions of generative phonology: the interplay of the alternation condition and the relatedness condition as criteria for rule plausibility. In a now classic paper P. Kiparsky (1968b) proposed the elimination of what he called absolute neutralizations as a condition of underlying representations. Accordingly, analyses which represent segments which do not appear phonetically in any environment are to be excluded. The intended effect of the condition was to constrain the theory of generative phonology in such a way that runaway abstraction and free-wheeling practices would not be possible. I will show that Kiparsky's alternation condition cannot produce the intended effect without a further condition of 'paradigmatic relatedness' on underlying representation.

Note in fact that in principle the theory allows as plausible rules any formulation based on two 'phonetically (etymologically) and semantically' related forms with the help of diacritic lexical features. It is possible under these stipulations to write a phonology of English which includes rules of languages like Romance as well as other languages, as long as there are no absolute neutralizations and the lexicon is properly stratified. It is theoretically impossible, therefore, to distinguish on language-internal basis whether a rule is a rule of English or not.

I proposed that 'paradigmaticity' is a further restriction on Kiparksy's alternation condition. In other words, if the scope of a phonological rule is limited to a particular paradigm, say the first conjugation o-stem verbs in Spanish, then the alternation condition applies to forms within that paradigm only. Accordingly, the phonological analysis which represents leveled diphthongs in first conjugation verbs in Chicano would constitute a case of absolute neutralization, and would be excluded from the set of plausible analyses.

The effect of a 'paradigmatic relatedness condition' coupled with the 'semantic and phonetic relatedness' plus Kiparsky's alternation condition significantly impoverishes the capacity of the theory and provides a morphological criterion for rule plausibility.

The definition of the paradigmatic condition hinges on the definition of what constitutes a paradigm. Obviously, 'paradigm relatedness' is defined within each language, and is amenable to empirical study within the present state of linguistic research, to a degree that 'semantic relatedness' is not. Here I can offer only a program without a conclusive solution.

It seems, for example, that verb forms in general are more closely related among themselves than they are with noun forms (we have observed leveling occurring in verb forms but not in noun or other forms). It seems also that forms of subparadigms of the verb have a closer degree of relatedness. It seems to me that if we paired forms in different grammatical categories, we would arrive at a gradience scale of paradigmaticity (a 'squish' in Ross's latest study in nondiscrete grammars) to be used as a criterion for rule plausibility in generative phonology.

In conclusion, I have shown that a characterization of the phonology of Chicano Spanish is amenable to two fundamentally different solutions: one phonological, the other morphological. I have argued that the phonological analysis is untenable on the basis of its implicit predictions about the nature of linguistic change and linguistic theory. By contrast, analogical leveling of diphthongs has a natural characterization as lexical restructuring, perfectly consistent with a theory of linguistic innovations. For the subjunctive phenomenon, two possible analyses appear plausible, one morphological, the other syntactic; but the choice between the two awaits further empirical data.

I have argued, in conjunction with the analyses, that the present theory of generative phonology allows free use of rules which vastly extends the power of the grammar and allows all kinds of crazy analyses across the languages of the world. I have informally proposed a condition of 'paradigmatic relatedness' which, coupled with Kiparsky's alternation condition, greatly reduces the power of the grammar and serves as a phonology-independent measure for rule plausibility.

REFERENCES

Harris, J. W. 1973a. On the order of certain phonological rules in Spanish. In: A Festschrift for Morris Halle. Ed. by R. Anderson and P. Kiparsky. New York, Holt, Rinehart and Winston.
_____. 1973b. Spanish stress rules revisited. Paper read at the LSA winter meetings, San Diego, California.
_____. 1974a. Morphologization of phonological rules: An example from Chicano Spanish. In: Linguistic studies in romance languages. Ed. by J. Campbell, M. Goldin, M. Wang. Washington, D.C., Georgetown University Press.
_____. 1974b. Stress assignment rules in Spanish. In: 1974 Colloquium on Spanish and Portuguese Linguistics. Washington, D.C., Georgetown University Press.
Kiparsky, P. 1968a. Linguistic universals and linguistic change. In: Universals of linguistic theory. Ed. by R. Harms and E. Bach.
_____. 1968b. How abstract is phonology? Indiana University Linguistics Club. Mimeo.

THE FREE-RIDE PRINCIPLE
AND THE SO-CALLED IMPERSONAL SE

MARGARITA SUÑER

Cornell University

Abstract. In dealing with the problem of impersonal se in Spanish three linguists, Roldán (1971), Langacker (1970), and Schroten (1972) have used A. Zwicky's (1970) Free-Ride Principle as a device to achieve economy of description. Each one bases his analysis on the assumption that impersonal se's can be derived in the same manner as reflexive pronouns, thereby creating structures which can get a free ride on the independently motivated Reflexive rule.

Both semantic and syntactic arguments are presented showing that impersonal se should be kept separated from other se's, even if this might require introducing impersonal se as a participle.

The conclusions confirm Zwicky's in that the Free-Ride Principle may be enticing, but it should be handled cautiously.

In his paper 'The Free-Ride Principle and Two Rules of Complete Assimilation in English', Zwicky (1970:579) states that:

> The following situation occasionally arises during the process of constructing partial grammars: A number of rules present themselves, and these alternatives are indistinguishable, or nearly so, from the point of view of formal simplicity; however, if a particular candidate R_1 is chosen, the domain of applicability of some independently motivated rule R_2 will be increased when R_1 is ordered before R_2. According to an oft-used methodological rule of thumb (the Free-Ride Principle), the analyst should choose this candidate (and get a 'free ride' on R_2).

132

Zwicky then proceeds with some arguments for and against the principle while presenting a few preliminary examples. After a detailed analysis of two morphophonemic rules for English, he argues (1970: 579) that 'they cannot serve as examples of the Free-Ride Principle, which (in general) lacks convincing support.'

This Free-Ride Principle has been appealed to by others with respect to a specific problem in Spanish, that of the impersonal se. The purpose of this paper is to discuss the treatment of the impersonal se in Spanish as presented by Roldán (1971), Langacker (1970), and Schroten (1972), and to show that these hypotheses are inadequate. The only motivation for their proposals seems to depend on the application of an independently well-motivated rule, the Reflexive transformation, which provides the basis for a free ride for their various postulations.

In the first part the three presentations themselves are discussed in detail to bring out the formal anomalies necessary for the application of the reflexive rule to impersonal se sentences. The second part deals with the semantic differences while the third part contributes some syntactic evidence which shows that impersonal se is nonreflexive.

1.   The presentations favoring the Free-Ride Principle

1.1.   Roldán (1971) characterizes the verbs that allow the impersonal se construction as: (a) transitive; (b) having a nonhuman object; and (3) requiring a human or at least an active subject. This latter active subject is underlyingly an indefinite ProN [+Human] which never gets filled lexically and therefore becomes deleted by transformation. Some of her examples are:

(1)   (R 17.6)[1]   Se alquila un cuarto.
                     'Room for rent.'
(2)   (R 17.7)   Se hacen camisas a medida.
                 'Shirts made to measure.'
(3)   (R 17.9)   Se compran botellas.
                 'Bottles bought here.'

In keeping with the framework of standard transformational theory, se is treated as a pronominal noun phrase and is inserted into the phrase marker by a transformational rule. Roldán (1971:28) gives the derivation for sentence (3) as:

(3a) underlying structure:

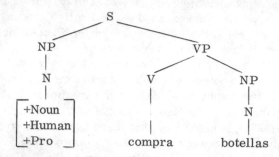

The NP under S, besides having the features for both noun and pronoun, is required to be [+Human]. No mention is made as to whether
it needs to be plus or minus indefinite, in spite of her (1971:24)
statement that 'these sentences have an "understood" underlying
indefinite active subject: in syntactic terms, an underlying indefinite
ProN [+Human] subject . . .'

The first transformation that applies to the foregoing underlying
structure is:

(3b) subject substitution

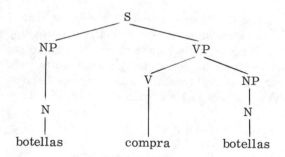

which transports a copy of the object NP into subject position. This
is a very questionable transformation. Attention should be drawn to
the fact that a nonlexicalized NP with the features [+Noun, +Human,
+Pro] is somehow replaced by a lexicalized NP characterized as
[+Noun, -Human, -Pro]. Such is the case of botellas. Not only
does the value of the feature Human mysteriously change, but the
original Pro node is filled with a copy of a true noun. Roldán
writes (1971:24) that

. . . the superficial subject of all these sentences is their
underlying object. These sentences have all the properties

of normal passives, although they appear in the active reflexive
form.

Her belief that impersonal se sentences are passives with deep structure objects manifested as surface structure subjects may be inferred
to be one of her motivations for postulating the Subject Substitution
transformation.[2] But her strongest motivation seems to be provided
by the next step in the derivation. Subject Substitution yields as its
output the structural description required for the application of the
Reflexive rule.

(3c) reflexivization

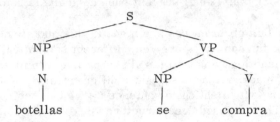

This rule transforms the second of two identical NP's into the
clitic se. Two additional transformations are postulated by Roldán
in order to produce the surface sentence (3): they are Subject-Verb
agreement (which, in this case, makes the verb plural, compran)
and Subject Extraposition (which extraposes the NP subject to a position after the verb).

Thus, by creating the very questionable Subject Substitution transformation, Roldán has its output take a free ride on the independently
motivated Reflexive rule.

1.2. Langacker (1970) in his review of Goldin's book, Spanish
Case and Function, criticizes the complexity of the rules as opposed
to the fairly narrow range of data they account for. Therefore, he
sets out to construct less complex rules which will generate the same
sentences. The framework is that of case grammar.

For the purposes of this paper I discuss the treatment of only the
reflexive pronouns. Goldin derives the following three sentences by
means of three distinct rules:

(4) (L 31) Se mató 'He killed himself.'
(5) (L 32) Se quejó 'He complained.'
(6) (L 33) Se trabajó 'One worked.'

Sentence (4) is derived by the True Reflexive rule, sentence (5) by the Automatic Reflexive rule and (6) by the Reflexive Pronoun Insertion rule.[3]

Although my primary interest is (6), which is an impersonal se sentence, Langacker's observations (1970:176) about all these sentences given are the following:

> It is by no means obvious that a single rule can account in a natural way for all three types of reflexives, for (31)-(33) are very different from one another semantically. Nevertheless, one would certainly prefer an analysis that led, as an automatic consequence, to a unified treatment of sentences like (31)-(33), and I shall suggest such an analysis below.

Two important observations are made in this quotation: first is the claim that the sentences are very different semantically (and I might add syntactically as well), and second that a 'unified treatment' (in spite of the acknowledged semantic differences) is desirable.

By directing our attention to sentence (6) we can see how Langacker derives it. The proposed deep structure is:

(6a) (L 61) trabajó AGENT

where AGENT represents an unspecified Agent. Langacker (1970: 182) clarifies it:

> Although an unspecified Agent will not normally be manifested in surface structure, I have adopted a derivational constraint[4] to the effect that the presence of an unspecified Agent or Dative in deep structure must have some effect at the surface level. Given the rules under discussion, the Agent in (61) will leave a trace in surface structure just in case Subject Choice 1 applies, but not Subject Choice 2.[5] Subject Choice 1 derives (62) from (61).

(6b) (L 62) AGENT trabajó AGENT

And the derived structure (6b) gets a free ride on the Reflexivization rule, thus obtaining (6).

Taking this derivation as an illustration, we see that Langacker, in an effort to provide a unified treatment for semantically different sentences, has had to resort to: (a) a derivational constraint, and (b) the identity of two empty nodes. The questions that come to mind are: Is it worth it? What has been gained? It seems that the only gain is the application of the Reflexive transformation and that only at a very high cost. Instead of restricting the power of the theory, derivational constraints have the opposite effect; they open an enormous realm of possibilities. And 'if descriptive power is enormous, the theory is rather uninteresting . . .' (Chomsky 1970). Moreover, Langacker's derivational constraint cannot be justified solely on the basis of this unspecified Agent (and Dative) case. The derivational constraint is adopted for one very specific syntactic description; adoption of such a powerful device is not supported in any independent cases by Langacker and it must therefore be suspect as being a convenience and nothing more. Derivational constraints should not be accepted without questioning their validity. Furthermore, the establishment of identity among empty nodes is undesirable, especially when other alternatives are available. [6]

A rule for Object Substitution is proposed by Langacker (1970: 178) as:

A copy of an inanimate Objective may be substituted for an unspecified Agent or Dative in subject position.

According to Langacker:

(7) (L 73) Se rompieron las ventanas con un martillo
              'The windows were broken with a hammer. '

has the following deep structure:

(7a) (L 74) rompió AGENT las ventanas con un martillo

Subject Choice applies yielding:

(7b) (L 75) AGENT rompió las ventanas con un martillo

(7b) qualifies for Object Substitution:

(7c) (L 76) las ventanas rompieron las ventanas con un
              martillo

To which the Reflexive rule applies, producing sentence (7).

Observe that the Object Substitution transformation operates identically to Roldán's Subject Substitution, i. e. it replaces an Agent, a nonlexicalized NP that must have (at least) the features [+Noun, +Pro] and [+Human] or [+Animate] with a lexicalized NP which is characterized as [+Noun, -Pro] and [-Human] or [-Animate].

Langacker himself writes (1970:183):

The reader may rightly be somewhat skeptical about the rule
of Object Substitution. Although it allows us to generate the
desired sentences by means of the regular Reflexive rule,
the whole thing looks like a trick.

But because Langacker thinks that Object Substitution is well motivated, I would like to examine the reasons he gives to support it.
First, he says (1970:183) that Object Substitution 'allows us to avoid
an apparent anomaly in the subject choice hierarchy'; this is because
in example (7) 'the Objective (ventanas) has been chosen as subject
despite the presence of an Instrumental (martillo)' (1970:183). This
argument is itself a debatable one. For example, I have discussed
elsewhere (Suñer 1973 and forthcoming; see also Otero's articles)
that a NP like ventanas is not the subject of a sentence like (7). The
only reason some seem to think it is a subject is because it agrees
with the verb which is also in the plural form. In view of the existence of sentences like:

(8) Habían muchas personas en la fiesta.
     'There were many persons at the party.'
(9) Llovieron piedras.
     'It rained stones.'
(10) Hacen tres años que no la veo.
     'It is three years that I haven't seen her.'

which are truly subjectless sentences in which the objects, being
plural, cause the verb to pluralize (object-verb number attraction),
it is not unreasonable to postulate that ventanas also causes the
optional pluralization of the verb romper 'to break'. From the
example:

(11) Se rompe las ventanas con un martillo.
     'One breaks the windows with a hammer.'[7]

we can get sentence (7) by a very late optional agreement rule.
     Langacker gives a second motivation for his Object Substitution
transformation. He tries to justify it by drawing attention to the
similarities between the se and the passive construction. He says
(1970:184), 'Reflexive sentences like (73) can be used in lieu of the
passive construction . . .' This statement is, at best, inexact. It
is prompted in part by equating an English gloss with the meaning
of the Spanish sentence and in part by the assumption that a sentence
like (7) (L 73) is basic instead of derived (in this case from (11)).

Moreover, it is not true that reflexive sentences can be substituted for passives. Compare, for example:

(12) ¡Ahora se prepara la tarea y no se mira la televisión!
'Now one prepares the homework and (one) does not watch TV!'
(13) ??¡Ahora la tarea es preparada y la televisión no es mirada!
'Now the homework is prepared and the TV is not watched!'

Or Bull's examples (1965:269):

(14) Se rompe 'One is breaking it. It breaks.'
(15) Es roto 'It is broken.'

Neither sentences (12) and (13) nor (14) and (15) can be used interchangeably. The sentences with se have a sense of immediacy and of imperfectivity that is effectively blocked by the past participle of the true passive sentences.

In conclusion, Langacker's rule is unmotivated. The attempt to reduce all instances of se to one derived through Reflexivization is enticing but completely unfounded.

1.3. One should also examine Schroten's 1972 study written within the case grammar framework as well. We can see how he accounts for the data considered up to now. Schroten is aware of Langacker's 1972 proposal (1972:39) and the solutions are parallel.

Schroten distinguishes five normal types of pseudoreflexive sentences:

(16) (S 1b) Se vende el libro.
'The book is sold' or 'One sells the book.'
(17) (S 3b) Se adora al héroe.
'The hero is adored' or 'One adores the hero.'
(18) (S 5b) Se busca un criado.
'A servant is being looked for' or
'One is looking for a servant.'
(19) (S 7b) Se ve que el chico trabaja.
'It is seen that the boy works' or
'One sees that the boy works.'
(20) (S 9b) Se baila 'One dances.'

As was the case for Langacker, the discussion will be limited to the types of examples given as (16) and (20). Schroten uses the term pseudoreflexive for what we call impersonal se. As in Langacker, he also uses Goldin's treatment of impersonal se sentences as a point of departure, and he also arrives at the conclusion that it will be desirable to derive this impersonal se in the same way other reflexive pronouns are derived.

He gives two arguments (1972:37) for his choice:

First, it is clear that most of the traditional grammarians share the intuition that some way or another the se of pseudoreflexive sentences is a reflexive pronoun. Secondly, we make a stronger claim by introducing se as a reflexive pronoun than by introducing it as a participle.

Although Schroten terms the above as 'arguments', I doubt they provide support for his choice. First, to do what others have done is not an argument per se; and in the second 'argument' he does not explain what he means by a 'stronger' claim. Why is it stronger? We can surmise that he means stronger because it appears to provide an explanation for why se, and not any other word, should appear in impersonal sentences. But we will see, as was the case with both Roldán and Langacker, that he does not give well-motivated support for collapsing of both se's. What he does is to create a derived structure which will get a free ride on the Reflexive rule.

Schroten comments (1972:39):

In order to derive the se of pseudoreflexive sentences in the same way (i. e. as reflexive se), we should only formulate a transformational rule which causes the derived structure of pseudoreflexive sentences to meet the structural description of (77), i. e. Reflexive rule. That is, we have to derive a structure in which the subject is identical with some other noun phrase.

But in order to formulate this transformation, which is the T-pseudoreflexive, Schroten has to make several assumptions:

(21a) He has to modify Fillmore's case grammar so that 'Proposition' is always expanded into 'Agentive' and 'Predicate'.

(21b) He has to postulate cases having no phonetic realization (mainly because he requires that at least one case must be present in deep structure).

(21c) He assumes that identity of empty nodes is possible.

(21d) He necessitates the postulation of three different Agentives: normal Agentives, fully unspecified

Agentives [+Human, -Specified], and formal Agentives
[-Specified].

(21e) He needs to assign rule features to the verbs to ensure
the application or nonapplication of certain rules (dele-
tions, T-formal reflexive I, among others).

His T-pseudoreflexive reads:[8]

(22) (S 154)
Fully unspecified human Agent + V + Objective
$\Longrightarrow$ Objective + V + Objective

that is, it replaces the fully unspecified human Agent by an Objective.
The underlying structure for (16) is given as:

(23) (S 159)

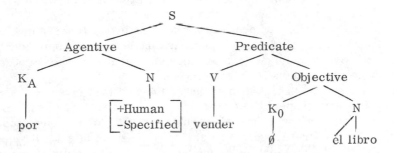

By applying T-pseudoreflexive the [+Human, -Specified] Agentive
Noun is replaced by the [-Human, -Animate, +Specified] Noun (phrase)
el libro. The validity of this type of transformation has already been
discussed.

Then, by application of the reflexive, the subject preposition
deletion, and subject extraposition rules, the surface sentence (16)
is arrived at.

The deep structure of (20) is:

(24) (S 184)

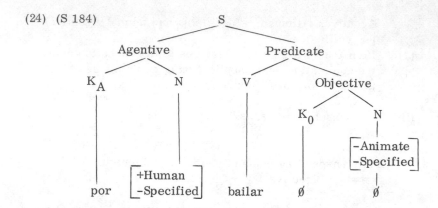

In this case T-pseudoreflexive replaces the unspecified human Agent by an unspecified inanimate Objective Noun. T-reflexive will establish identity of two nonlexicalized nouns and insert the se;[9] then, T-subject preposition deletion and T-subject extraposition will apply, rendering the surface structure sentence (20).

In conclusion, by positing T-pseudoreflexive (itself a questionable transformation), Schroten increases the domain of applicability of the Reflexive transformation, but does so only at the expense of (at least) those assumptions listed under (21).

To summarize, I have reviewed the positions taken by three linguists with respect to impersonal se sentences in Spanish. All three posit a transformation (call it Subject Substitution, Object Substitution, or T-pseudoreflexive) which achieves the same effect. It replaces a nonlexicalized Agent (or a subject NP) with a lexicalized inanimate object. The main motivation for the postulation of this rather ad hoc transformation seems to be to provide the structural description required for the application of the Reflexive rule.

Moreover, both Langacker and Schroten resort to the questionable practice of positing identity between two empty nodes. In view of the advances in and the need for constraining the power of the theory, such unconstraining devices as identity of nonlexicalized nodes, derivational constraints, and rule features should not be accepted without question.

2. Semantics

Implied in the three analyses I examined is the claim that impersonal se and reflexive se are identical. But all of the analyses assume distinct underlying structures for sentences such as (25) and (26):

(25) (S 80) Juan se mató
　　　　　　 'John killed himself' (or 'John died').

(26) (S 81) Se mató a Juan.
'(Some)one killed John' (or 'John was killed').

hence distinct semantics as well. This implied claim is even more
absurd when one takes into account that Schroten argues in favor of
keeping impersonal se sentences separate from true reflexives (in
spite of his derivations) because of the differences between the surface structures and the semantic interpretations as exemplified in
(25) and (26). Semantically impersonal se implies an unspecified
Agent (or Experiencer) while the true reflexive se refers back to the
Subject of the sentence.

The main point is that these se's represent not only lexical
ambiguity but syntactic ambiguity as well. By neutralizing deep
structure differences in order to allow the Reflexive rule to apply to
the derivations, ad hoc constraints are applied to derived structures
in order to achieve this goal (Schroten's rule features and Langacker's
derivational constraint).

3. The syntactic evidence

Really strong evidence for keeping impersonal se and reflexive se
apart would be any demonstrable differences in the syntactic behavior
of the two se's. This would indicate that speakers know the two are
different because some rule (or rules) would apply to one of them and
not to the other. This kind of evidence does exist. A sentence like
(27):

(27) Juan se afeita todas las mañanas.
'John shaves himself every morning.'

may be embedded in another sentence

(28) Miro a Juan afeitarse todas las mañanas.
'I watch John shave himself every morning.'

In (28) the subject of the embedded sentence (Juan) is transformed
into an object marked with the preposition a; the verb, left without
a subject, takes the infinitive form, and the reflexive se is attached
to the infinitive.

But if one attempts to perform the same operation with an impersonal se sentence:

(29) Se conversó mucho en esa reunión.
'One talked a lot in that meeting.'

the result is an ungrammatical sentence

(30) *Oigo conversarse mucho en esa reunión.

Someone might object that the ungrammaticality of (30) is not only due
to the infinitive + impersonal se sequence but also due to the fact that
(29) is a subjectless sentence. These objections are easily countered
by the following examples in which subjectless constructions can
nevertheless be embedded.

(31) Llueve 'It rains. '
(31a) Oigo llover 'I hear it raining. ' [lit: 'I hear to rain']
(32) Nieva 'It snows. '
(32a) Parece que quiere nevar 'It seems that it wants to snow. '

The crucial issue is the impossibility for an impersonal se to occur
with an embedded infinitive. [10] Two other examples will illustrate the
point further. For sentence (34a) the reflexive reading is possible
(although weird), whereas the impersonal interpretation is not.

(33) Se toca la guitarra de 3 a 5.
       'One plays the guitar from 3 to 5. '
(33a) *Quisiera tocarse la guitarra de 3 a 5. '
(34) En este restaurante se come con los dedos.
       'In this restaurant one eats with one's fingers. '
(34a) En este restaurante hay que comerse con los dedos.
       'In this restaurant one has to eat oneself with one's fingers. '

but not

       *In this restaurant one has to eat with one's fingers. '

The different syntactic behavior of the two sentences with respect to
infinitives shows that they must be maintained as two separate
entities, because the difference could not be explained if both se's
resulted from the application of the same rule.
    There is another instance in which the se's act differently, at
least for some speakers. [11] Ramsey (1956:106 and 388) notes that
les is to be expected instead of los when the clitic is masculine
plural and preceded by the impersonal se. He illustrates the point
with example (35).

(35) Eran tan pocos que apenas se les hubiera creído capaces
       de atacar un castillo medianamente fortificado.

'They were so few in number that one could hardly have
thought them able to assault a castle only tolerably forti-
fied. '

An example I would like to add is the following:

(36) Se $\begin{Bmatrix} \underline{les} \\ *\underline{los} \end{Bmatrix}$ esperó durante horas.

'One waited for them for hours.'

Mark Goldin in a personal communication suggests that the principle
seems to work even with the masculine singular form. He offers this
example:

(37) No sé que ha pasado con Jorge, pues no <u>se</u> $\begin{Bmatrix} \underline{le} \\ *\underline{lo} \end{Bmatrix}$ ha
visto últimamente.
'I don't know what's the matter with George--no one
has seen him lately.'

While <u>le/les</u> is required with the use of impersonal <u>se</u>, no such
requisite is established for the reflexive <u>se</u>, i.e. reflexive <u>se</u> + <u>los</u>
can cooccur.

(38) Juan <u>se</u> <u>los</u> llevó todos.
'John took them all with him.'
(39) (Él) Se <u>los</u> lavó con una substancia nueva.
'He washed them himself with a new substance.'

Consequently, examples (35-39) show that some speakers intuitively
make a distinction between impersonal <u>se</u> and reflexive <u>se</u>, which
supports my criticism of those who want to derive both <u>se</u>'s by means
of a common rule.

4. Conclusion

In view of the foregoing discussion it seems quite apparent that
there is no justification, formal, semantic, or syntactic, for deriv-
ing the impersonal <u>se</u> by means of the Reflexive rule; consequently
impersonal <u>se</u> should be derived independently.
The conclusions of this paper confirm Zwicky's findings that the
Free-Ride Principle looks very enticing and that in the absence of
conclusive evidence it might be preferred over several indistinguishable alternatives. But as soon as new evidence is brought to bear
on a solution that uses this rule of thumb, the predictions made by
the principle might prove to be incorrect, and it should be discarded.

NOTES

*My gratitude to Erik Beukenkamp, Mark Goldin, and Arnold Zwicky for their valuable comments on an earlier version of this paper. Nevertheless, all errors remain my own.

1. Henceforth the letter followed by a number will indicate the example number of the original author's work.

2. Space prevents me from expanding this point but see Suñer (1973 and forthcoming), and Otero's articles for more detailed discussion.

3. Goldin's rules read:

True Reflexives: (69) When there are identical noun phrases within a sentence, one of which is the subject, the one which is not the subject takes the form of a reflexive pronoun.

Automatic Reflexives: (81) If a verb is present which requires a reflexive pronoun, one is inserted.

Reflexive Pronoun Insertion: (22) If an Agent is not present but potentially could be, and if (7b) did not apply, or if an Agent is not potentially present with a verb that permits Dative subject, then a reflexive pronoun is inserted.

4. Langacker's derivational constraint (1970:178-9) reads: Constraint on derivations: If a deep structure contains an unspecified Agent or Dative, then any surface structure derived from it must differ in some way from the surface structure that would be derived from the corresponding deep structure lacking the specified element.

5. Subject Choice (1970:178): 'One case element is transported out of the proposition and placed in superficial subject position: the order of priority is Agent, Dative, Instrumental, Objective.' Later on Langacker (181) divides this rule into two processes: copying and deletion. 'Implicit in any transportation rule, therefore, is the possibility of a derived structure containing two occurrences of the element being transported: this will come about whenever the first step is taken but the second is blocked for some reason.'

6. Two alternatives come to mind. Impersonal se could be introduced transformationally in the VP of the sentence, or it could be generated directly by the phrase structure rules of the base component. (See Suñer 1974 for an elaboration of this latter alternative.)

7. The gloss of (11) is also valid for (7).

8. The more precise formulation of T-pseudoreflexive (Schroten 1972:65) is:

$$K_A + N \begin{bmatrix} +\text{Human} \\ -\text{Specified} \end{bmatrix} + V + K_0 + N + X$$

SD: 1　　2　　　　3　　　4　　5

SC: 1, 2, 3, 4, 5 $\implies$ 1 + 4, $\emptyset$, 3, 4, 5

9. This seems to be in contradiction to Schroten's own T-reflexive (1972:96) which reads: 'If in a sentence there are two NP's referring to the same entity and having the same lexical representation, and if one of the NP's is the subject of that sentence, then the NP that is not the subject will take the form of a reflexive pronoun.'

10. There are examples where impersonal se occurs with an infinitive.

(i) Al anunciársele a Juan el resultado le echaron chispas los ojos.

Sentence (i) is synonymous with:

(ii) Cuando se le anunció a Juan el resultado le echaron chispas los ojos.

The English gloss is the same for both of these sentences: 'When one announced the result to John, his eyes sparkled.' However, the way in which (i) and (ii) are derived is beyond the scope of this paper.

11. The differentiation does not apparently correspond to the division between the 'leístas' and the 'loístas', because I have encountered some 'loístas' who required the les with the impersonal se.

REFERENCES

Bull, William E. 1965. Spanish for teachers: Applied linguistics. New York, The Ronald Press Co.
Chomsky, Noam. 1970. Some empirical issues in the theory of transformational grammar. Mimeo. Indiana University Linguistics Club.
Goldin, Mark. 1968. Spanish case and function. Washington, D.C., Georgetown University Press.
Langacker, Ronald. 1970. Review of Spanish case and function by Mark Goldin. Lg. 46.1.167–85.
Otero, Carlos P. 1966. El otro se. Reprinted in C. P. Otero's Letras, I. London, Tamesis.
_____. 1972. Acceptable ungrammatical sentences in Spanish. Linguistic Inquiry 3.233–42.
_____. 1973. Agrammaticality in performance. Linguistic Inquiry 4.551–62.
Ramsey, Marathon M. 1956. A textbook of modern Spanish. Revised by R. K. Spaulding. New York, Holt, Rinehart and Winston.

Roldán, Mercedes. 1971. Spanish constructions with se. Language Sciences 18.15-29.

Schroten, Jan. 1972. Concerning the deep structures of Spanish reflexive sentences. Janua Linguarum, Series Practica, 173. The Hague, Mouton.

Suñer, Margarita. 1973. Nonparadigmatic se's in Spanish. Unpublished doctoral dissertation, Indiana University.

_____. 1974. Where does impersonal se come from? In: Linguistic studies in romance languages. Washington, D.C., Georgetown University Press.

_____. (forthcoming). Demythologizing the impersonal se in Spanish. Hispania.

Zwicky, Arnold. 1968. Naturalness arguments in syntax. Chicago Papers.

_____. 1970. The Free-Ride Principle and two rules of complete assimilation in English. Chicago Papers.